P9-DUV-592

THE ATLANTIC CONNECTION

PHILIP H. TREZISE

THE ATLANTIC CONNECTION
Prospects, Problems, and Policies

THE BROOKINGS INSTITUTION
Washington, D.C.

D
1065
.U5
T73

Copyright © 1975 by
The Brookings Institution
1775 Massachusetts Avenue, N.W.
Washington, D.C. 20036

Library of Congress Cataloging in Publication Data:

Trezise, Philip H   1912–
    The Atlantic connection
    1. Europe–Relations (general) with the United States.
    2. United States–Relations (general) with Europe.
    3. North Atlantic Treaty Organization.
    4. European cooperation.
    I. Title.
D1065.U5T73   327.4'073   75-19321
ISBN 0-8157-8527-5

9 8 7 6 5 4 3 2 1

Board of Trustees

Douglas Dillon
Chairman

Louis W. Cabot
Chairman,
 Executive Committee

Vincent M. Barnett, Jr.
Lucy Wilson Benson
Edward W. Carter
George M. Elsey
John Fischer
Kermit Gordon
Huntington Harris
Roger W. Heyns
Luther G. Holbrook
William McC. Martin, Jr.
Robert S. McNamara
Arjay Miller
Barbara W. Newell
Herbert P. Patterson
J. Woodward Redmond
H. Chapman Rose
Warren M. Shapleigh
Gerard C. Smith
Phyllis A. Wallace
J. Harvie Wilkinson, Jr.

Honorary Trustees

Arthur Stanton Adams
Eugene R. Black
Robert D. Calkins
Colgate W. Darden, Jr.
Marion B. Folsom
John E. Lockwood
John Lee Pratt
Robert Brookings Smith
Sydney Stein, Jr.

THE BROOKINGS INSTITUTION is an independent organization devoted to nonpartisan research, education, and publication in economics, government, foreign policy, and the social sciences generally. Its principal purposes are to aid in the development of sound public policies and to promote public understanding of issues of national importance.

The Institution was founded on December 8, 1927, to merge the activities of the Institute for Government Research, founded in 1916, the Institute of Economics, founded in 1922, and the Robert Brookings Graduate School of Economics and Government, founded in 1924.

The Board of Trustees is responsible for the general administration of the Institution, while the immediate direction of the policies, program, and staff is vested in the President, assisted by an advisory committee of the officers and staff. The by-laws of the Institution state: "It is the function of the Trustees to make possible the conduct of scientific research, and publication, under the most favorable conditions, and to safeguard the independence of the research staff in the pursuit of their studies and in the publication of the results of such studies. It is not a part of their function to determine, control, or influence the conduct of particular investigations or the conclusions reached."

The President bears final responsibility for the decision to publish a manuscript as a Brookings book. In reaching his judgment on the competence, accuracy, and objectivity of each study, the President is advised by the director of the appropriate research program and weighs the views of a panel of expert outside readers who report to him in confidence on the quality of the work. Publication of a work signifies that it is deemed a competent treatment worthy of public consideration; such publication does not imply endorsement of conclusions or recommendations.

The Institution maintains its position of neutrality on issues of public policy in order to safeguard the intellectual freedom of the staff. Hence interpretations or conclusions in Brookings publications should be understood to be solely those of the authors and should not be attributed to the Institution, to its trustees, officers, or other staff members, or to the organizations that support its research.

63964

FOREWORD

Almost thirty years after World War II the U.S.-European connection remains at the center of American foreign policy. The U.S. commitment to the North Atlantic Treaty Organization has more influence than any other single factor on the size and character of U.S. general purpose military forces; action on key economic problems—inflation, recession, and oil prices—hinges on U.S.-European-Japanese cooperation; and prospects for U.S.-European agreement help to shape American policy on a wide range of international political issues.

To say that the U.S.-European connection is important does not tell us much about its future prospects. The recriminations exchanged between the United States and Europe after the Arab-Israeli war in October 1973 led to predictions that the Atlantic alliance was entering a fatal decline; more optimistic views were expressed when the Atlantic countries adopted a unanimous if innocuous declaration at the Ottawa meeting in June 1974. In August 1974, the Cyprus crisis renewed European criticism of U.S. policy and despondency about NATO's future; but in December 1974 the Franco-American agreement at Martinique led to greater cheerfulness about Atlantic prospects, as did the 1975 NATO summit meeting.

Such passing moods and events inevitably distort perception of longer-term trends and underlying problems. Philip Trezise, a senior fellow at the Brookings Institution with extensive previous experience in relations among the developed countries as U.S. ambassador to the Organisation for Economic Co-operation and Development and as assistant secretary of state for economic affairs, undertook the analysis of the Atlantic connection and its future presented here in consultation with Guido Colonna di Paliano, former member of the Commission of the European Community and former deputy secretary-general of NATO. Mr. Trezise did so at the request of Senator Jacob K. Javits, chairman of the Committee of Nine, a group of prominent Europeans and Americans formed in 1971 to make recommendations about Atlantic policy to the North Atlantic Assembly.

Since submitting his preliminary conclusions to the committee, the author has refined and elaborated his study, taking account of recent events. After examining a wide range of issues and problems he concludes that the trans-atlantic system is likely to survive the crises of the future as it has those of the past, and that the political skills and capacities possessed on both sides of the Atlantic are great enough to sustain and strengthen a relationship that remains central to the prospects for peace and progress throughout the world.

Philip Trezise wishes to acknowledge his debt to colleagues at the Brookings Institution—particularly to Edward R. Fried, Henry Owen, and Jeffrey Record—for advice and comment, and to Senator Javits and other members of the Committee of Nine for their insights and encouragement. The study was made possible by a grant from the Ford Foundation; the manuscript was edited by Barbara P. Haskins.

The views presented are those of the author. They should not be attributed to the Ford Foundation, to the Committee of Nine, or to the trustees, officers, or other staff members of the Brookings Institution.

KERMIT GORDON
President

June 1975
Washington, D.C.

CONTENTS

CHAPTER ONE

INTRODUCTION

The October 1973 war between Israel and its Arab neighbors produced a major crisis in U.S.-European relations. Americans resented the lack of European support for what they considered to be wise policies for dealing with the energy problem and for strengthening peace in the Middle East; while Europeans resented what they saw as a lack of consultation, brusque tactics, and the unduly pro-Israeli policies of the United States.

One reason for these differing reactions was the differing circumstances of the two regions at that time: the United States since 1947 had identified with Israel to a greater degree than the European countries; the latter had in the same period become more dependent than the United States on oil exports from the Arab nations. But another reason lies in deep-seated trends: the European countries' criticism of U.S. policy was aggravated by their belief that the United States, while still professing its dedication to collective goals, was becoming increasingly nationalistic and insensitive to Europe's concerns. And American resentment of that criticism was intensified by the view that the European nations, while emphasizing their independence of the United States on a wide range of issues, seemed incapable of effective joint action—even in those areas (for example, defense) where they professed an identity of interest with the United States.

These views, in turn, reflected the fact that the United States and Western Europe are passing through contrasting and difficult transitional periods. The United States, trying to adjust to a relative decline in its world position, is preoccupied with domestic problems, only to find that these are powerfully shaped by external events that can no longer be controlled without the cooperation of other industrial nations—notably those in Europe and Japan. Western Europe can no longer readily provide that cooperation; while the era in which weak and disunited European nations were willing to accept U.S. leadership unquestioningly is now over, Europe has not yet become a strong community

1

capable of concerted action on its own. This gap between America's perceived need for Europe to play a strong role and the reality of European weakness and division provides fertile ground for mutual disenchantment whenever a major crisis, be it in the Middle East or the economic arena, creates a need for effective Atlantic response. The difficulty is compounded by the fact that the needs to which joint action would be addressed are no longer as evident as in the cold war period.

As a result, the Atlantic Ocean has seemed to be growing wider—not narrower. The question is whether this will continue and, if so, where it will lead. It does not take much imagination to see how these trends could decisively compound tensions in a U.S.-European relationship that is already troubled by economic disputes and by the differing perspectives that often produce cool and skeptical European responses to U.S. initiatives. Strident European criticism of U.S. policy in the Cyprus crisis only underlines how easy it is for a clearly recognized common problem to lead to dissension rather than unified action.

However, such recent setbacks need to be viewed in a historical perspective. The Atlantic relationship has functioned reasonably effectively in defense, in nearly all economic areas, and in most East-West dealings for a quarter-century. Apart from the absence of general war, this may be the single most important achievement of the postwar period. And it may help to explain some other significant characteristics—the relative stability of Central Europe and the rapid expansion of economic growth in the industrial world—that distinguish this period from the era between World Wars I and II.

An effective U.S.-European relationship was not inevitable; indeed, prewar experience suggested that it was unlikely. That a good relationship was maintained for a generation may be even more surprising, in any long-term perspective, than the problems currently facing the alliance. For the Atlantic crisis is a recurring one; since the Suez debacle of 1956, pundits on both sides of the Atlantic have periodically predicted the demise of the Atlantic relationship. It has been a rare year in the past two decades that has not seen intellectuals in both Europe and the United States proclaim that the two regions stand at the crossroads.

The question, then, is not whether the alliance faces serious problems; it surely does. The question is whether the long-term trends discussed above preclude or obviate the need for concerted Atlantic action; and, if not, what changes in existing policy are necessary if the U.S.-European relationship is to serve useful ends.

Solutions are not self-evident. Past successes may have little relevance for the future. And the recent record is mixed. To determine whether today's problems are unique—and maybe insoluble—requires an examination in depth of U.S.-European relations. And to be fruitful, this examination must focus not on general principles but on specifics. For it is the pattern of action and inaction in dealing with hard problems that will determine the future of Atlantic relations.

In *defense,* the future of the common system of the Atlantic nations for maintaining European security is uncertain. Some questions to be raised are fundamental: for example, is that system still needed in an era of détente and rising European strength? Others are more limited: in light of changes in the relative roles of the United States and Europe toward any external threat, how should the burdens of defense be distributed and its efficiency improved?

In *politics,* debate focuses on whether joint Atlantic policies still make sense and are feasible. The quest for security agreements in Europe between East and West poses a basic issue: the United States has unilaterally pursued a policy of rapprochement with the Soviet Union (and with China); and the European nations, alarmed by this despite U.S. assurances, have wondered whether they should not follow suit. Another concern is policy toward third areas of the world and whether the whole idea of concerted Atlantic action is realistic or impossible because of conflicting U.S. perceptions of the needs in such areas as the Middle East.

In *economics,* the international order, which was devised largely by the countries of North America and Western Europe, and which had much to do with their unprecedented prosperity, is now challenged by opposing ideas of national and regional advantage and by an unexpected rise in the world price for petroleum. Can the existing order be revised and adapted to new conditions or is the basic concept of a global economic order based on the principle of comparative advantage now obsolete because of these new conditions?

This paper commences with a general review of the postwar period of close transatlantic relations, Soviet policy, and intra-European trends and is followed by a detailed examination of the problems mentioned above. Then the principal transatlantic issues and possible outcomes are considered, and the paper concludes with an appraisal of the Atlantic relationship and some suggestions regarding its future direction.

CHAPTER TWO

A HISTORICAL PERSPECTIVE

In 1919 John Maynard Keynes returned from the Peace Conference in Paris to write these forlorn words:

But if, as we must pray they will, the souls of the European peoples turn away this winter from the false idols which have survived the war that created them, and substitute in their hearts for the hatred and the nationalism, which now possess them, thoughts and hopes of the happiness and solidarity of the European family—then should natural piety and filial love impel the American people to put on one side all the smaller objections of private advantage and to complete the work, that they began in saving Europe from the tyranny of organized force, by saving her from herself. And even if the conversion is not fully accomplished, and some parties only in each of the European countries have espoused a policy of reconciliation, *America can still point the way and hold up the hands of the party of peace by having a plan and a condition on which she will give her aid to the work of renewing life.*[1]

In the event, as Keynes surely must have expected would be the case, the European peoples hung on steadfastly to their historic quarrels and suspicions, and America went its mainly indifferent way. Ironically, private American lenders did in time make the large contribution to European recovery that Keynes had hoped for, but in a wholly apolitical context. Officially the United States played a part in the disastrous economic settlements made at Versailles by insisting on war debt payments, which in turn depended on the payment of reparations by Germany. And of course the United States returned to its traditional political isolation and to a somewhat less traditional trade policy of protectionism.

For Western Europe, the twenty years between the two world wars were merely an interlude in the European civil conflict. By the mid-thirties, the hopes for a durable peace in Europe had been shattered, and a new war was imminent. Meanwhile, political absolutism existed in much of Europe, and

1. John Maynard Keynes, *The Economic Consequences of the Peace* (Harcourt, Brace, and Howe, 1920), p. 285. (Emphasis added.)

except in Scandinavia and the British Isles democratic political institutions seemed generally to be in mortal danger. And in the aftermath of the Great Depression, the European economy was split into national bits and pieces, at enormous cost in efficiency and welfare.

The Post-World War II Era

Against this dreary background the post-1945 experience is remarkable. Unlike the quasi-divorce that took place between the two sides of the Atlantic after 1919, the period since World War II has been one of unprecedented cooperation in military, political, and economic matters. In the Marshall Plan and later through the North Atlantic Treaty, the United States voluntarily assumed a leading role in Atlantic affairs, which has continued, though in lesser degree, to the present. Institutions were created and formal procedures developed for conducting transatlantic affairs. After twenty-eight years, in which immense changes have occurred around the world, the close relationship between the United States and Canada and the countries of Western Europe remains a major element in the ordering of international affairs.

At various times during the post-World War II years, the objectives and the interests that impelled the Atlantic nations to cooperate received differing emphases. Nevertheless, it is useful to recall that a succession of political leaders on both sides of the Atlantic had quite specific, interlinked objectives that their policies were intended to serve.

• A first and major purpose, which today is sometimes almost forgotten, was to eliminate as completely as possible the causes of war in Western Europe—mainly the power rivalry between France and Germany.

• A second, which is reflected in the North Atlantic Treaty, was to assure the security of all the Atlantic countries against the great military power of the Soviet Union.

• A third purpose was to preserve democratic political processes in Western Europe.

• A fourth was to recover economically from the devastation of World War II and to create the foundation for enduring prosperity.

• And finally, from the Marshall Plan on, there was the continuing aim of eventual coalescence of the Western European nations into a European political and economic entity.

Peace within Western Europe

Viewed in perspective, the pursuit of these goals has been remarkably successful. Peace among the nations of Western Europe is now taken for granted.

No one seriously believes that a resurgence of rivalries and ambitions on the scale that led to general wars in 1914 and 1939 is possible. France and Germany are to all appearances permanently reconciled. For the first time since Charlemagne, it is hard to imagine a conflict arising in the western half of the European continent. This is a development of major importance that now goes almost unnoticed, so accustomed are we to it.

The peace today in Western Europe can be attributed to the devastation of World War II, to the subsequent war weariness of the Western European peoples, and to the rise of superpowers with military capacities that are far beyond the reach of ordinary states. But it is also in part attributable to a political leadership that set out deliberately to create habits of thought and institutional forms that would work to prevent a renewal of the near-suicidal national rivalries of the past. The postwar politicians who had foundations to build on proceeded to do so with vigor and skill.

East-West Tension

Although peace within the West can be taken as a durable fact, peace between Western and Eastern Europe obviously can not. Large military forces with armaments and weapons of enormous destructive power are deployed in Central Europe; in Eastern Europe major political issues arising out of the conflict between Soviet dominion and local nationalism remain unsettled. Soviet military power, moreover, extends into the North Atlantic and the Mediterranean, where it meets forces of the North Atlantic Treaty Organization (NATO). It would be foolish to deny that this situation has latent, if no longer urgent, dangers within it.

Yet, as François Duchêne has said, peace in all of Europe today is strong, not weak.[2] Although all potential sources of conflict have not been eliminated and may not be in this century, an accommodation has been achieved—as a result of an effective balance of power—that makes conflict unattractive to all concerned. Some revisionist historians in the United States now say that there never was a Soviet military design on, or threat to, Western Europe and that the cold war was in effect a U.S. invention for U.S. imperialist purposes. This reading of events that included, among others, the blockade of Berlin and the 1948 coup in Czechoslovakia will not appeal equally to everyone. In any case, the United States decided at the end of the 1940s to involve itself by treaty in the security of Western Europe, and in due course it became a major partner in the North Atlantic alliance. By so doing, it made certain that the Soviets

2. François Duchêne, "A New European Defense Community," *Foreign Affairs,* vol. 50 (October 1971), pp. 69-82.

could take no military action against Western Europe with the hope of assured and inexpensive political or territorial gains. The situation created then still exists today—more than twenty years later.

To be sure, the European military scene has changed. While the original strategic deterrent remains, though now in the form of a rough balance between the United States and the USSR in nuclear destructive power, there is a confrontation of conventional military forces in Europe, which at least makes uncertain the outcome of any armed attack. This uncertainty is greater because both sides have extensive tactical or short- and medium-range nuclear weapon capabilities.

Better ways of insuring against war are not hard to imagine. The balance in Europe is not only one of terror and uncertainty, but, like the global strategic balance, it is liable to the risks of human misjudgment and, what would be worse, irrational behavior. But if an "era of negotiation" is now truly under way, it can fairly be said to reflect to an important degree the existence of that balance—an accomplishment of the Atlantic system and a further reason for having confidence in the strength of European peace. The treaties negotiated by the Federal Republic of Germany (FRG) with the USSR and Poland and the conferences on European security and on mutual force reductions indicate a still tentative and partial recognition that there is no logical alternative to discussion and negotiation concerning the shape and future of Europe. That recognition on the part of the leaders of the USSR surely must be attributed in some measure to the patience, forbearance, *and* evident determination of the partners in the Atlantic relationship.

Western Europe Today

A quarter of a century ago, the concern was not only that the Soviet Union might apply overt military pressure against Western Europe; there was also a fear that the political scene on the European continent would be dominated by the communist parties in Italy and France. Having emerged from a war that ended the rule of totalitarian governments of the Right, Europe then seemed distressingly likely to succumb to totalitarianism of the Left. Nothing of the sort has happened. The politics of the Western European states in the 1950s and 1960s may not always have been models of orderly procedure; France, for example, had a close brush with civil strife over the settlement of the Algerian conflict. But the dominant political themes have been continuity and respect for popular choice and representative government. The communist parties in France and Italy remain, but their revolutionary fervor has diminished. Turkey, Greece, Spain, and Portugal have been exceptions to this general rule that democratic institutions are basically strong in Western Europe. But the long-term trend in Spain seems to be toward somewhat greater political freedom, and events in Greece during the summer of 1974 offered similar hope.

At all events, Western Europe as a whole does not appear in imminent danger of succumbing to antidemocratic governments. There is political turbulence and tension, due in part to rapid inflation, but there is also an apparent feeling that popular elections are the way to resolve differences and to set the basis for policies. If there is a likelihood that authoritarian regimes of the Left or Right will soon come to power in the European democracies, it is not readily apparent. In France, for example, noncommunist political parties of both Left and Right try hard to persuade the electorate that they are forces of the Center; in Italy, the communists—whose participation in government is being discussed—profess to be supporters of the European Community (EC);[3] in Germany the Social Democrats are in power, thanks to a coalition with a free enterprise party.

The Years Ahead

All this could change, of course. Continuing inflation at recent rates might undermine the political structure by radicalizing the middle classes or by convincing majorities that democratic governments simply cannot be effective. These may be valid fears, particularly in the countries worst hit by the current recession and the international effects of the energy crisis. Ranged against them, however, is the record of a quarter-century of continuing reliance on democratic procedures and elected governments. The claim that democracy is in peril must be based on stronger evidence than the experience of such a brief period.

The moderation of European politics to date has been in no small part a result of postwar European prosperity. The most striking feature of the postwar years has perhaps been persistently high employment; the steady and, by past standards, rapid growth of incomes; and the absence of depression or severe economic fluctuations. This has been the situation in both Western Europe and North America. It underscores a critical difference between the interwar years and the period since 1945. After World War II, nearly all the Western governments consciously took responsibility for assuring high levels of employ-

3. *EC* actually stands for "European Communities" or "European Community." It is the collective name for the European Coal and Steel Community, the European Economic Community, and the European Atomic Energy Community. Belgium, France, Italy, Germany, the Netherlands, and Luxembourg were founding members. The United Kingdom, Ireland, and Denmark joined on January 1, 1973 (European Community, *The Facts* [European Community Information Service, February 1974]).

ment and economic prosperity. They then found or developed techniques for carrying out these commitments, not perfectly but adequately. In spite of the evident inability of governments to accomplish all desirable economic objectives (price stability has eluded every country), and in spite of the difficult adjustments and declining rates of growth brought on by energy shortages and the higher prices of oil, we can expect in most Western European countries the degree of material well-being needed for political pluralism. Looking beyond the present crisis, on the economic front the main long-term threat is not that growth will lag unduly but that its benefits will be limited and their distribution distorted by endemic inflation, which can have powerful adverse political effects. On the record to date, that inflation will continue and will be the most serious threat to economic well-being and political moderation in Western Europe. The strains that inflation puts on people in the middle and fixed income brackets are clearly threatening social cohesion. It is not even certain that democratic institutions as firmly rooted as those in Britain can withstand the shock of severe inflation.

Inflation is one reason why changes in total output, or even in levels of employment, do not tell us everything about changes in welfare or human contentment. The gross national product figures do tell us, however, that the peoples of the Western countries have had at their command a constantly increasing quantity and variety of goods and services. Taken as a whole, they are within easy range of ending poverty, as the term is defined in any absolute sense. There are, of course, physical and environmental costs associated with such economic growth. But the skills and productive capacity are available to deal with these costs, once the political will to do so has been generated.

The healing in the postwar years of Western Europe's most fundamental internal divisions has gone hand in hand with a trend toward a closer and more institutionalized association of the Western European states. The erratic course of this movement toward European integration, which is discussed at some length in chapter 4, should not obscure the progress that has been made since 1945. Early notions, in the United States particularly, about the prospective rapid development of a federal political entity in Europe took far too little account of the difficulties of overcoming the deeply embedded and diverse national attitudes and aspirations that marked and still mark Western Europe. Setbacks and disappointments have been inevitable, given the overly high expectations.

From another, and possibly more reasonable perspective, the European image is quite different. The European Community, in its role as a limited customs union, has survived; indeed it has prospered and expanded. Even as the six-member European Economic Community, it was a compelling force in the world; witness its attractiveness to nonmember nations in Europe, in Africa, and even in more distant areas. The admission of other countries has enhanced this appeal.

Agreement on the *content* of Europe will be immensely more difficult, of course, and there will be further crises and setbacks in the political evolution of the region. But one would have to be blind not to see how much has happened and how far Europe has moved from being a region of separated and contending states, as it was for all of modern history. Even if European unity goes no further than a customs union and a free trade area, it will be a major force in shaping the Atlantic relationship.

European Relations with North America

Over the years, relations between North America and Western Europe have gone through a succession of trials. From the beginning, the postwar decolonization process carried within it the makings of major differences between Europe and the United States; yet virtually all of the colonies became independent, with much less upheaval than might have been expected, and transatlantic differences on this point have not left an enduring residue. When the European Defence Community failed in 1954, the promised American "agonizing reappraisal" was brief and not in any sense apocalyptic.

In the 1956 Suez episode, the United States openly broke with two of its principal Atlantic allies on an issue that Britain and France considered important enough to justify the use of military force. Yet the Atlantic connection continued. A decade later General Charles de Gaulle took the French armed forces out of NATO and asked the NATO establishment to leave France. At the same time the United States was launching a military effort in Vietnam, from which its allies remained aloof and which in time some of them came to deplore publicly. Neither General de Gaulle's actions nor the unpopularity of the Vietnam War destroyed the Atlantic system. This recital could be continued indefinitely if we were to take into account all of the misunderstandings and differences—military, political, and economic—that have afflicted the Atlantic relationship and have been overcome or adequately managed throughout the postwar years.[4]

4. The hazardous state of the relationship has constantly preoccupied its close observers. See, for example, Henry A. Kissinger, *The Necessity for Choice: Prospects of American Foreign Policy* (Harper and Brothers, 1960), chap. 3, for comments on the situation at the end of the Eisenhower administration; Theodore C. Sorensen, *Decision-Making in the White House: The Olive Branch or the Arrows* (Columbia University Press, 1963), chap. 3, for comments on the Kennedy administration; and Curt Gasteyger, *Europe and America at the Crossroads* (Paris: The Atlantic Institute, 1972), for a contemporary assessment.

On many of the occasions when the relationship came under special strain, purposeful steps were taken to relieve the pressure. The military alliance would probably not have come through the 1960s as well as it did if NATO strategy had not been debated and revised, or if the United States had not decided to share with its allies knowledge about the issues surrounding the nuclear deterrent. Similarly economic relations between North America and the European Community might have worsened to an unacceptable degree if it were not for the energies expended in completing the Kennedy Round of trade negotiations and the efforts that were devoted to consultation or negotiation on problems arising out of the increasingly close links among the Atlantic economies.

At various points, moreover, the leaders of the Soviet Union provided pointed reminders that, in the intra-European confrontation, the position of Eastern European countries is, in fact, different from that of the NATO allies and that Soviet power is real and usable. The lessons of East Berlin, of Hungary, and of Czechoslovakia clearly did not overwhelm the growing Western European desire for détente; but along with periodic alarms over West Berlin and the increasing presence of Soviet military strength outside Eastern Europe, they served as a warning that the defensive aspects of the Atlantic relationship had meaning and purpose after all.

Hence, strong forces have impelled the Atlantic powers to deal with problems as they arise. These forces reflect some more or less common culture and value systems, a similar—although not identical—perception of possible threats to national and regional security, and a growing, if not always fully understood, economic interdependence.[5] Their existence has tended to draw the Atlantic nations together, even when powerful divisive pressures were at work. Whether this will continue to be the case, as the Atlantic connection changes in the face of new trends, or whether the Atlantic nations will henceforth elect to follow more separate political, military, and economic paths, will depend both on domestic trends within these countries and on how certain pressing external problems are handled.

5. "It could even be said that what were once the principal objectives of sovereign powers—the maintenance of economic prosperity and of effective defense—can now only be achieved by the acceptance of cooperative international arrangements which by their very nature impose limitations on the sovereignty of all the nations concerned." William McChesney Martin, *Toward a World Central Bank?* (International Monetary Fund for the Per Jacobsson Foundation, 1970), p. 21.

See also Richard N. Cooper, "Economic Interdependence and Foreign Policy in the Seventies," *World Politics,* vol. 24 (January 1972), pp. 159-81, for a thoughtful discussion of the economic ties linking the Western industrial countries and of the difficulty of translating economic interdependence into political reality.

The Distribution of Power

Common to all the issues discussed here is the dilemma of the changing balance of power. After World War II the disparity of power between the United States and Western Europe enabled the United States to mobilize the resources of the Atlantic countries for common purposes in the military, economic, and—to some extent—political fields; what were described as Atlantic programs and institutions were, in many cases, shaped in Washington. Now the disparity between potential U.S. and European power has been diminished by the revival of Western Europe. Theoretically the remedy would be to redistribute responsibility within the Atlantic relationship. But in practice this is difficult to do. Most of the effective postwar international institutions owe their success to the accepted de facto dominance (or, more euphemistically, leadership) of one power. There is still no evidence that, as U.S. leadership recedes, efficient international management will take its place. There are divisions within Europe, and economic issues have emerged that pose special problems for international management. For example, failure of the attempt to achieve monetary reform and the resort to floating exchange rates instead show that, in some cases, the answer may be to accept a slowing or even a reversal of the trend toward interdependence. In the political field, differing U.S. and European reactions to the Middle Eastern crisis illustrate the point even more vividly. The problem is compounded by the increasing emergence both of transnational actors, whose activities sometimes escape government control, and of differing ideas of the role and responsibility of government in the United States and Europe.

The key questions, in the face of these trends, are whether common action is still required and, if so, whether new means can be found to achieve it. Before considering these questions, however, it is useful to review the role of a major actor whose policies will do something to shape the answers: the USSR.

CHAPTER THREE

THE SOVIET UNION AND EASTERN EUROPE

To the outside observer, the Soviet Union appears in two guises. From one perspective it is a military superpower, with the second largest economy in the world and a political system that has endured for half a century in the face of immense upheavals and trials. It is firmly in command of its Eastern European neighbors and fully determined to remain so. It exerts influence throughout the world. And its institutions enable it to establish foreign policy goals without the distractions of public debate and to pursue them with a flexible but determined strategic purpose.

Another view, however, sees an inefficient, badly overstrained economy that is unable to meet all the demands put on it by the military arm, by its goal of rapid economic growth, and by its long-deprived consumers. Pressures for internal change continue and cannot be ignored entirely. The political system is maintained by repression and can confer legitimacy on its rulers only by maneuver and intrigue within a small clique of Communist party veterans. It is a country with many minority nationalities, most of whom are potentially restive under the Great Russians. Its European allies are resentful and politically uncertain enough to require a Soviet military presence or threat to assure their stability and reliability. It is engaged in a bitter struggle with China that carries within it the threat of a major war. Its ventures outside Europe have been costly and by no means uniformly successful. Its internal policymaking apparatus seems to be just as creaky as those of Western governments but has far more extensive and complex tasks to perform.

Both views are accurate, at least in part. The idea of the USSR as a monolith, at home and in the communist world, has been greatly eroded by events. It is more than twenty years since Stalin's death, and far-reaching changes have taken place in the Soviet Union, in Eastern Europe, and in the USSR's relations with other powers. Yet the pattern of change over that period is not one of discontinuity. Unrest within the USSR and within Eastern Europe has been successfully contained. Troubles—in the Soviet economy, in relations between the USSR and the Eastern European countries, and in Sino-Soviet affairs—are systemic, but they are familiar troubles. There is no convincing evidence that the Soviet view of the world has undergone any fundamental shift, nor does any sharp break with the past appear likely. The prevailing structure of institutions seems to have good prospects for survival.

The Soviet Domestic Scene

In little more than half a century, the USSR has survived the most extraordinary ordeals: civil war, collectivization of its farms, famine, the Communist party purges of the 1930s, and a devastating war. Yet the political and administrative structure that was created, mostly in the 1920s, to rule and manage this immense and diverse country remains intact today and essentially unchanged. It is evident that there must be strong forces making for stability in the Soviet system.

The principal characteristics of that system stem directly from the initial decision, in line with Russian tradition, to give to the state the monumental and complex task of determining in detail the country's productive activities. Having rejected market forces as at least a partial means of deciding what should be produced and how, there was no escaping the need for a huge bureaucracy. For the Soviet system to function, not only must it have the extensive bureaucratic machinery that every modern state has—for defense, for social and health services, for justice, for foreign affairs, for public utilities— it also needs a vast officialdom to direct and operate in large and small detail virtually the entire economy.[1]

Left to its own devices, this army of bureaucrats would have brought anarchy. Each interest group, whether military, industrial, or agricultural, would have been in unrestrained competition for its "share" of the nation's productive capabilities. So it is the Communist party leadership, exercising political direction and control, that makes the system work. The leadership must decide what will be available to the military, to heavy industry, to agriculture, and to the consumer, and how these shares will be produced. It must then set in motion and guide the decisionmaking process, down to minor choices at local and factory level.[2] And to ensure that the central decisions are carried out, it infuses into the bureaucratic and administrative machinery,

1. Merle Fainsod, *How Russia Is Ruled* (Harvard University Press, 1953), chap. 17.

2. The system, of course, is not and could not be operated in the degree of detail that a pure theory of centralized planning would require. In the real world, a great many decisions must be made outside the planning process. But a centrally planned economy, Soviet-style, does depend on bureaucratic and political controls to an extent that goes beyond Western experience, even wartime experience. See Alex Nove, *The Soviet Economy: An Introduction* (second ed., Praeger, 1969).

at key points, officials who are party members, and thus subject to the discipline and incentives that the party provides.[3]

Moreover, choices made in the early years inescapably led the Soviets to the use of repression and police control. Rapid industrialization required sacrifices from the Soviet people that could be obtained only through compulsion. The collectivization of agriculture, while a logical action under the Soviet dogma, called for the massive use of force.[4] Habits and institutions formed or perfected then have endured ever since.

Out of all this a system has emerged that is cumbersome, overcentralized, and by Western standards quite inefficient. The people who control and operate it are aware of some of its weaknesses. And debate about these weaknesses does go on. At the same time, millions of party members and key nonparty people get perquisites, privileges, and power from the system, which they might lose if it were to be altered in any basic way. Their interests lie in the status quo, or something close to it. Above all, they are not likely to favor change that would upset established procedure or threaten their positions.[5] This large vested interest in stability is a reason, more important than the influence of Marxist doctrine, for supposing that change will come only slowly to the Soviet Union.

In the abstract perhaps there is no overriding reason why the political controllers of a centrally directed economy could not allow a wide measure of intellectual freedom, of access to the outside world, and even of popular participation in the political process. Since the death of Stalin, indeed, the trend in the Soviet Union has been toward relaxing controls.[6] But in a community where repression, and for long periods massive oppression, has been a standard way of governing, the risks of liberalization must seem immense.[7] The doc-

3. Fainsod, *How Russia Is Ruled,* chap. 17.

4. Winston Churchill quotes Stalin as having said that the stresses of collectivization were as great as those of World War II. *The Second World War: The Hinge of Fate,* vol. 4 (London: Cassell, 1951), pp. 447-48.

5. Khrushchev undertook major reorganizations of the bureaucracy and the party control structure in 1957 and in 1962. These were overturned after his removal from office and seem to have been in part the cause of his downfall. See Michel Tatu, *Power in the Kremlin,* English translation by Helen Katel (London: Collins, 1969), pp. 249ff.; and Gertrude E. Schroeder, "Economic Organization and Management as Factors in Soviet Economic Growth in the 1970s," in *Prospects for Soviet Economic Growth in the 1970s,* Main Findings of Symposium held April 14-16, 1971, at Brussels (Brussels: NATO Information Service, 1971), pp. 147-56.

6. "Every Soviet citizen feel[s] that he is living in greater security and enjoying more personal freedom than he did fifteen years ago. . . ." Andrei Amalrik, *Will the Soviet Union Survive Until 1984?* (Harper and Row, 1970), p. 27.

7. Even in nations with long democratic traditions, it may be noticed that governments are seldom wholly at ease with the activities of dissident citizens or the press.

trine as interpreted does not provide for it, and experience is against it. Further-more, the heterogeneous character of the Soviet population is a reason for caution; the Union may be in no danger of disintegrating, but the loyalty of its many minority nationalities can hardly be taken for granted.[8] To relax controls precipitately or wholesale might weaken the structure of the Soviet state.

It follows that political liberalization will come slowly, whether or not there exists the immutable Russian tendency to tyranny that some observers see.[9] Soviet experience and the structure of the Soviet state and politics make it unlikely that the country will move soon to any recognizable form of inter-nal political libertarianism. If the Russian environment and Russian history add strength to these forces, then the end to a fundamentally repressive and closed Soviet society may be far off indeed.[10]

This is not to ignore the various pressures on Soviet leaders to mitigate the rigors of an inordinately centralized and undemocratic regime. Discontent over low standards of living has been a continuing cause for concern. If the various nationalities in the Soviet Union cannot wholly be trusted, neither can they be ignored; it may even be that the poorer areas of the Soviet Union have benefited through sizable resource transfers from the richer regions pre-cisely because of the leadership's concern over restiveness in non-Russian areas of the country.[11] The small band of brave people who are willing to speak out publicly against the regime seems regularly to be replenished, in spite of the harsh treatment meted out by the authorities.[12] As its foreign trade has expanded, and as the country's external interests have grown, more and more Soviet citizens are being exposed to the outer world.

Within the regime itself there is disagreement, argument, and discussion. A relapse to the paranoid dictatorship of the Stalin years is unlikely and probably would not be allowed to continue for long if it happened. By the standards of the Soviet past, the direction of change has been toward greater

8. Robert Conquest, *Soviet Nationalities Policy in Practice* (London: Bodley Head, 1967).

9. "The Russia of Custine and Herberstein, of Olearius and Fletcher, of Von Staden and Madame de Stael is almost indistinguishable from the Russia of today. Fifty-four years of Communism has done little to change it. . . ." John Dornberg, *The New Tsars: Russia Under Stalin's Heirs* (Doubleday, 1972), p. 447.

10. It is noteworthy that Amalrik's vision of the collapse of the Soviet state (in *Will the Soviet Union Survive?*) is based on an anticipated war with Communist China.

11. See Herbert S. Dinerstein, "The Soviet Outlook," in Robert E. Osgood and others, *America and the World: From the Truman Doctrine to Vietnam* (The Johns Hopkins University Press, 1970).

12. Dornberg, *The New Tsars,* chap. 3.

freedom and a more open society. Unfortunately, those standards are very low and the distance to go very great.

At some time during the 1970s, in all probability the USSR will once more face the problem of succession to leadership. The Communist party's General Secretary, Leonid Brezhnev, is in his late sixties and presumably will have to be replaced before the end of this decade. No formal or legal procedure exists for determining the succession; if history repeats itself, the next general secretary will establish himself in that position by a series of deals and maneuvers, or purges, through which he will eliminate or reduce in status his principal rivals. So it was with Stalin and then Khrushchev, and so has it been with Brezhnev.

An internal contest for power in the Soviet Union is thus likely to take place within the fairly near future. Recent precedent tells us that it will be mainly nonviolent in character. Still the chances of domestic upheaval and radical change in policy some time during the decade are high, as a new leadership seeks to consolidate its authority over the Communist party and other elements in Soviet society. This is a situation for which there is no appropriate analytical model. But the prospect that the highest positions in the party (and thus the roles of power in the country) will be open for new occupants is bound to affect the internal political process and every key decision in the years ahead.

The Soviet Economy

From the Western point of view—and the Soviet as well—the question about the USSR's economy in this decade is: can it support an unchanged or growing defense program, provide for rising levels of civilian consumption, and keep investment at the very high levels that have enabled the country's GNP to grow in the past decade at rates much like those achieved in Western Europe?

The answer is a considerably qualified yes, for there are serious conflicts among Soviet economic objectives. The desire to improve the lot of the consumer, which is no doubt genuine, is in competition with the requirements for industrial growth. Either the consumer or the industrial investment sector, or both, could benefit from reduced spending on defense. Moreover, the economic system has been performing rather poorly, even by Soviet standards, and is in need of innovations or reforms that might increase productivity.[13]

13. See Stanley H. Cohn, "General Growth Performance of the Soviet Economy," in *Economic Performance and the Military Burden in the Soviet Union,* A Compendium of Papers submitted to the Subcommittee on Foreign Economic Policy of the Joint Economic Committee, 91 Cong. 2 sess. (1970), pp. 9-17.

But these are the long-standing, chronic conflicts and problems of the Soviet economy. They do not at this time seem likely to compel the kinds of changes in priorities—especially a reduction in defense—that might affect the foreign policies of the USSR or its internal stability.

During the 1960s, the Soviet economy grew at a rate of about 5 percent a year, with annual figures fluctuating in accord with good and bad crops, for the USSR, despite its place as the world's second industrial power, is still very much an agricultural country. In 1972 total output, in current U.S. dollars, was about $550 billion, or roughly half that of the United States.[14] During the 1960s, per capita consumption rose by 41 percent;[15] in 1969, however, it accounted for only 55 percent of a GNP computed according to Western definitions.[16] Defense expenditures (in constant rubles) rose by more than 75 percent and were probably about 10 percent of GNP at the end of the 1960s. Investment, which grew more slowly than in the 1950s, took some 30 percent or more of the nation's output.[17]

If the Soviet Union could do about as well in the 1970s as it did in the 1960s, the regime presumably would find the results satisfactory, if not all that it had hoped. The Ninth Five Year Plan (1971-75) sets a target rate of growth for the GNP of 6 percent, with investment increasing at a rate of about 7 percent a year. If the target were reached, there would be room for substantial increases in consumption or, if desired, in defense expenditures—with of course tradeoffs between the two.

However, to attain the 6 percent goal would require greater increases in productivity than are likely to have been achieved.[18] Almost certainly the Soviet leadership will have to meet the various demands on the economy from a smaller-than-planned total volume of goods and services. Still a growth rate of, say, 5 percent, with investment increasing at the planned 7 percent rate, would allow per capita consumption to grow by 3 percent a year (lower than the 3.5 percent average for the 1960s and substantially lower than in 1965-69)

14. U.S. Department of State, Bureau of Intelligence and Research, "The Planetary Product in 1972: Systems in Disarray," Research Study, appendix, table 4.

15. David W. Bronson and Barbara S. Severin, "Consumer Welfare," in *Economic Performance and the Military Burden in the Soviet Union*, p. 97.

16. Terence E. Byrne, "Recent Trends in the Soviet Economy," in ibid., p. 6.

17. See Cohn, "The Economic Burden of Soviet Defense Outlays," in ibid., pp. 168-69; and "Summary of Discussions," in *Prospects for Soviet Economic Growth in the 1970s*, p. 15.

18. Douglas B. Diamond, "Principal Targets and Central Themes of the Ninth Five Year Plan," in Norton T. Dodge (ed.), *Analysis of the USSR's 24th Party Congress and 9th Five-Year Plan*, pp. 47-53; also Cohn, "General Growth Performance of the Soviet Economy."

and the defense budget by 4 percent. A 3 percent annual gain in per capita consumption is respectable by international standards; the comparable figure for the United States during the 1960s was 2.5 percent. For the Soviet people, whose levels of consumption are estimated to be one-third those of Americans, it might seem less adequate. But the regime would have margins within which to work to keep popular discontent under control, if that were necessary.

During the post-Stalin period, the regime has experimented with changes in the workings of the Soviet command economy. Major "reforms" were introduced in 1957 and 1962, and again in 1965.[19] They did not, however, effectively decentralize the decisionmaking process and clearly did not make the system notably more efficient. Resistance to basic change in the structure of party and bureaucratic control is bound to be stubborn. The host of functionaries with a stake in the status quo would be opposed, and so would many party leaders who were fearful of the ultimate consequences of radical change.

Some Western commentators, and perhaps a number of influential Soviet officials as well, believe that imports of foreign technology would significantly improve the efficiency of the Soviet economy. This is not an impressive proposition. While foreign machinery may help to break a bottleneck here or there, an economy that is spending $40 billion a year to create its own new industrial equipment, as the Soviet economy is, could not expect to solve its problems by adding a few billion dollars' worth of Western items, however advanced they were. More than one-third of the USSR's imports by value already consists of machinery and equipment. Even if priorities could be altered so as to increase this amount, the impact on productivity would not be decisive.

Again in principle, it might be possible to bring more people into the working force to compensate for lower rates of increase in investment. But for a number of reasons, including a probable unwillingness to further reduce the period of education for the young, this alternative offers little promise.[20]

There remains the defense sector. It takes up to 10 percent of the Soviet Union's current output, and the three million or so young men in the armed services constitute a reservoir of manpower for additional civilian employment. The military's share of GNP has fluctuated in the past and presumably will continue to do so. Because the Soviet military posture, and changes in it,

19. Another "reform," which would fit the country's industrial plants into a system of large corporations ("production associations"), was announced in April 1973. Reported in *New York Times,* April 8, 1973.

20. David W. Bronson, "Soviet Manpower Prospects in the 1970s," and M. E. Zaleski, "Problèmes de la main-d'oeuvre dans le neuvième plan quinquennal soviétique, 1971-75," in *Prospects for Soviet Economic Growth in the 1970s,* pp. 129-45 and 107-27, respectively.

have an important impact on world affairs in general, and the Atlantic relationship in particular, factors that affect Soviet defense spending are given closer examination.

Defense versus Civilian Needs

In the USSR, as in Western countries, the competition between defense and civilian uses for available resources is well recognized. As *Pravda* once put it:

On the one hand, it would be desirable to build more enterprises that make products for satisfying man's requirements, that produce clothing, footwear and other goods for improving people's lives. It would be desirable to invest more means in agriculture and to expand housing construction. . . . On the other hand, life dictates the necessity for spending enormous funds on maintaining our military power at the required level. *This reduces and cannot help but reduce the people's possibilities of obtaining direct benefits.*[21]

In virtually all Politburo discussions of domestic economic policy a debate over what resources will be allocated to defense must be implicit or explicit. One faction obviously reflects the professional and bureaucratic views of the armed forces, of the defense industry and its research and development apparatus, and of the proponents of emphasis on "heavy" industry.[22] The opponents would be those leaders who are especially concerned with keeping the consumer reasonably content, as well as those who see a conflict between defense spending and the objective of economic growth. In all normal circumstances, the outcome will be one of compromises over marginal amounts, with due concern for harmony within the ruling coalition. It is always possible, however, that in a time of economic stringency the choices to be made might put severe strains on the stability of the regime then in power.

Objectively the potential tradeoffs between reductions in the defense establishment and increases in consumption or investment seem to be rather modest. Cohn, for example, assumes that a reduction of 1 percentage point in the defense portion of GNP (and a shift of resources to investment) would translate into an increase of only 0.028 percent in the growth of total output.[23] That is to say, the cut in the defense share would have to be very great, down from 10 percent to just above 6 percent of GNP, to achieve a 1 percent increase in the rate of economic growth; this is not the kind of decision that

21. *Pravda* (Moscow), February 28, 1963, quoted in Vernon V. Aspaturian, "The Soviet Military-Industrial Complex—Does It Exist?" *Journal of International Affairs*, vol. 26, no. 1 (1972), pp. 3-4. (Emphasis added.)

22. Andrew Sheren, "Structure and Organization of Defense-Related Industries," in *Economic Performance and the Military Burden in the Soviet Union*, pp. 123-32.

23. Cohn, "The Economic Burden of Soviet Defense Outlays," in ibid., p. 179.

can be made on economic grounds alone. Even if, as is probably the case, the defense sector is considerably more efficient than Soviet industry as a whole, the transfer of defense industry skills and resources to other activities would take time, and in the process some of the higher productivity of defense workers would probably be lost. There is no easy way to make up systemic deficiencies in the economy by reallocating military resources.

As for the large pool of manpower in the Soviet armed services, it is but a small fraction of the USSR's total labor force of more than 120 million workers. The agricultural sector alone still accounts for 30 percent or more of the working population, a proportion far higher than in any other industrial country; as a potential source of industrial manpower it far outweighs the armed services.[24] While a really massive, one-time transfer of, say, a million soldiers to civilian life unquestionably would help to ease the Soviet Union through its temporary economic difficulties, it would not solve the basic problem of low productivity of both labor and capital in the USSR.

What emerges from this is familiar to all governments. Every faction in the debate can offer persuasive arguments. Advocates of the civilian economy can point to the large absolute amounts going to the military and the need for more resources in other sectors. The military group will cite external "threats" and perhaps also the genuine difficulties to be faced in converting defense resources to civilian use.

In these circumstances, the road to compromise is clear enough. Present plans seem to call for increases in defense spending at rates just below those of the increases in GNP. In other words, the plans call for a substantial rise in absolute terms—possibly one that Soviet leaders believe will improve their defense position relative to that of the United States by the end of the decade. Reducing the rate of increase would make some resources available to the civilian economy while the defense sector grew more slowly in absolute size. If diversions from the defense sector must be made, it would be entirely consistent with the conservative character of the present regime to take such a course; most unlikely would be reductions so large that they would provoke the military hierarchy to enter the political arena on behalf of a particular group of contenders for party control.

The competing claims for economic resources may well cause the Soviet leadership to look favorably on negotiations for further arms limitations and even reductions in forces. Gradual change is all that such negotiations imply, and that is what political leaders may consider feasible and safe. But in the end, it is very doubtful that economic considerations would be allowed to

24. Murray Feshback and Stephen Rapawy, "Labor and Wages," in ibid., p. 75.

determine the relative military position of the USSR. Policies that might threaten even remotely to undermine the nation's status as a great power would be unacceptable to the leadership and probably, for that matter, to the population at large. The problems of being one of the superpowers are real enough, but no one in authority or likely to be in authority in the USSR would think of opting for a lesser role in the world for the Soviet Union.

The USSR in Eastern Europe

From the final days of World War II up to the present, the unchanging element in Soviet foreign policy has been a perceived need to control Eastern Europe. Thus Soviet tanks were used in East Berlin in 1953. In the Polish Communist party crisis of 1956, Soviet military units were ostentatiously moved toward the chief cities of Poland as the political settlement was being negotiated. A few weeks later, the Red Army put down the Hungarian uprising. When Czechoslovakia's turn came in 1968, military power was again invoked.

If the use of armed force is the ultimate expression of external policy, then it must be assumed that Eastern Europe is highest among Soviet security concerns, after the USSR itself. After all, except for border skirmishes with China, the USSR has exercised its military capabilities since World War II only in Eastern Europe. We do not know how much risk the Soviets believed was involved when they intervened in Hungary or Czechoslovakia, but it could not have been judged to be zero. And Moscow certainly could not have disregarded the political costs of these actions, within the Communist movement and in relations with the West. It must be expected, therefore, that in similar circumstances the Soviet regime would again be ready to think of imposing its will and control through military action.

But this assumption takes us only so far. What would be similar circumstances? Both Yugoslavia and Albania have succeeded in breaking away from Soviet domination, although in the case of Yugoslavia future Soviet policy is still uncertain. Since the early 1960s Romania has conducted a foreign policy that is in large measure independent of Moscow. These were highly unwelcome developments that the Soviets accepted with evident displeasure, but accepted, at least for the time being, nonetheless. Hungary's experiment with economic liberalism has been tolerated, but the Czech experiment has not. The strikes and riots in Poland in 1970 were dealt with by conciliation and by changes in government and policy, rather than by resort to force (which might well have required the use of the Soviet troops stationed there).

Obviously there is no single pattern. The USSR is probably prepared to live with policies different, within quite wide limits, from its own—foreign policy, as in Romania, and domestic, as in Hungary or Poland. It cannot prevent the Eastern European states from expanding their trade and tourist ties with Western Europe. And after the settlements with West Germany, the Eastern Europeans have reason to argue for even more relaxation of Soviet control.

As Pierre Hassner comments, however, liberalization and toleration of differences cannot assure stability any more than total repression can be a workable permanent policy.[25] Nationalism evidently is more of a force in Eastern Europe than in Western Europe; its partial suppression seems only to give it strength. The communist governments are generally unpopular, except when they oppose Russian domination, as in Romania. Western Europe exerts a powerful attraction, culturally, economically, and finally politically; if the process of Western European unification goes well, this attractive power will increase. In a period of détente then the tendency in the satellite countries will be to take advantage of the relaxed environment and to go as far as possible in the direction of freedom from Moscow. Therein lies the abiding danger of threats to Communist party control, perhaps spreading rapidly from country to country and leading to military intervention—always with the possibility that armed resistance will be offered to the Soviet Army. It is not that a predictable threat to peace is seen in Eastern Europe, but rather that explosive forces will be present in the region just as long as the USSR's conception of its security interests calls for it to dominate the politics of its neighbors.

Yugoslavia presents a different hazard. Although doubtless Moscow has never reconciled itself to Tito's independent status, the Yugoslavian situation is a familiar one and by necessity tolerable, there being no apparent way short of war to change it. However, if the Yugoslav federation were to prove less cohesive after Tito's death or retirement, the opportunities for reviving Soviet influence there might be tempting to some members of the regime. This might be so especially if a contest for control were under way in Moscow, so that gains in Yugoslavia could be used for domestic political advantage. Speculation could go well beyond these rather standard observations. But it is perhaps enough to repeat the point that Hassner makes: *almost any evolution in Eastern Europe is possible except a harmonious one.*[26]

25. Pierre Hassner, "Europe East of the Elbe," in Robert S. Jordan (ed.), *Europe and the Superpowers: Perceptions of European International Politics* (Allyn and Bacon, 1971), pp. 74-100.
26. Ibid., pp. 99-100.

The USSR and Communist China

Presumably no aspect of intercountry relations is immutable. It must therefore be wrong to consider the break between the USSR and Communist China as beyond repair. However, a reconciliation between these two adversaries would seem to demand that one of them make fundamental concessions to the other's point of view; and at present no such concessions seem likely to be made.

Differences between the two countries are ideological, territorial, and racial. As Stefan Possony says, they concern matters that bear literally on survival.[27] The extraordinary ideological polemics in which both governments have indulged may be discounted in some measure as conventional vituperation between communist parties; Yugoslavia and the USSR had equally savage exchanges in 1948, and little Albania on occasion has scaled the heights of abuse in attacking the Soviet leaders; it is always possible to hope for a resolution of an ideological quarrel.[28] But at bottom the ideological dispute has grown out of a difference in view about relative positions in the Communist movement. The Soviet Union is unwilling to give up its claim to supremacy, and the Chinese are unwilling to grant it.[29]

Territorial issues between the two nations are at least as crucial as the ideological ones and offer even fewer prospects of mutually acceptable solution. Mao Tse-tung publicly laid claim in 1964 to some 1.5 million square kilometers of Soviet territory.[30] Soviet and Chinese soldiers have killed one another over the occupation of obscure points along the border between the two countries. The Soviet Union, for its part, argues that China's possessions in Sinkiang, Inner Mongolia, and Tibet are the loot of past imperial conquest[31] and should be disgorged.

The racial factor in Sino-Soviet relations is not a part of the public dialogue, but unquestionably it heightens the conflict. If dislike of the Chinese on racial grounds is as prevalent in European Russia as it seems to be,[32] similar attitudes must be found within the Soviet leadership. It is not hard to imagine

27. Stefan Possony, "Peking and Moscow: The Permanence of Conflict," *Modern Age*, vol. 16 (Spring 1972), p. 130

28. See Adam B. Ulam, *Expansion and Coexistence: The History of Soviet Foreign Policy, 1917-67* (Praeger, 1968), pp. 658ff. and 681ff.

29. See Michel Tatu, *The Great Power Triangle: Washington-Moscow-Peking* (Paris: Atlantic Institute, 1970), p. 12.

30. Ulam, *Expansion and Coexistence*, p. 693.

31. Possony, "Peking and Moscow," p. 137.

32. This prejudice has been noted by Western correspondents: Harrison E. Salisbury, *War Between China and Russia* (W. W. Norton, 1969), pp. 32-38; and Alberto Ronchey, *The Two Red Giants: An Analysis of Sino-Soviet Relations* (W. W. Norton, 1965), pp. 27-28.

how the idea of dealing with 800 million hostile Chinese might strike people who begin with a phobia about Orientals. Chinese attitudes toward the Russians undoubtedly are reciprocal.[33]

Whether Moscow at political levels ever considered taking preemptive military action against China may not be known until the Soviet archives are some day opened to examination.[34] There can be no doubt, however, that the *possibility* of a Sino-Soviet war has preoccupied both Moscow and Peking for the past several years. But neither country seems to have a wholly rational interest in starting such a conflict—China because of its relative weakness and the Soviet Union because a war with China might go on endlessly. Yet the mutual distrust between them has gone so far, and differences are so deep, that a genuine settlement seems to be out of the question, and a military conflict is always a possible outcome.

In this situation, which promises to be long-lived, the Soviet Union's external policies cannot fail to be affected by concern about China and the spread of Chinese influence in the world. The result will not necessarily, or even logically, be to constrain the Soviets from activism elsewhere, Soviet support for India, for example, has been motivated to a large extent by a desire to checkmate China in South Asia; and, as in the case of India, the pursuit of a policy intended to contain Chinese aspirations could bring the USSR into confrontation with the United States or the Western European countries. But, to sum up, it is undoubtedly true that Soviet policy toward Western Europe and the United States has been both modified and moderated by the threat of conflict with China, and this is likely to be a durable feature of the world scene.

The Middle East

Soviet external policy has a common thread—the pursuit of influence and power—but its application seems to be no less opportunistic and expedient than that of any other nation. At any rate, a broad strategic design is difficult to discern, except perhaps in the case of its policy toward Germany. Particularly in the third world, Soviet actions appear to be a series of ad hoc responses to events and seeming opportunities rather than to follow a consistent global policy. The lengthy, expensive, and basically hazardous investment of Soviet resources and prestige in Egypt apparently began at the initiative of the Egyp-

33. C. P. Fitzgerald, *The Chinese View of Their Place in the World* (London: Oxford University Press for the Royal Institute of International Affairs, 1964), pp. 57-64.

34. An attack on Chinese nuclear installations is widely reported to have been contemplated in 1969 after serious border clashes along the Ussuri River. Dornberg, *The New Tsars*, p. 248.

tians,[35] though it probably also reflected a Soviet tendency to view this area much as the United States has sometimes seen Latin America, or at least the Caribbean: as a geographically proximate region, in which its influence should naturally predominate. Nonetheless, in its tactics, the whole of Soviet Middle Eastern policy—from the pressures on Iran in 1946, through support in establishing the Israeli state, to Moscow's bluster at the time of Suez and the subsequent relationships with Egypt, Syria, and Iraq, as well as Soviet action in the 1973 Arab-Israeli war—all seems to have been largely opportunistic, even if basically expansionist.

Whatever may have been the specific motivations and objectives of the Soviets, they have obviously considered the establishment and preservation of positions in the Middle East to be important elements of external policy and to justify sizable expenditures and the placement of Soviet military forces far from their home territory. In particular, the presence of a Soviet fleet in the Mediterranean is the kind of foreign commitment that cannot easily be withdrawn. It is not necessary to describe this action in ill-defined terms, such as "outflanking NATO." It is, and is intended to be, visible evidence of Soviet power and Soviet interest, in line with Foreign Minister Andrei Gromyko's statement before the Supreme Soviet in June 1968:

The Soviet Union is a great power, situated on two continents, Europe and Asia—but the range of our country's international interests is determined not by its geographical position alone. . . .

The Soviet people does not plead with anybody to be allowed to have its say in the solution of any question involving the maintenance of international peace, concerning the freedom and independence of the peoples and our country's extensive interests.

This is our right due to the Soviet Union's position as a great power.

During any acute situation, however far away it appears from our country, the Soviet Union's reaction is expected in all capitals of the world.[36]

Gromyko's rhetoric no doubt should be appropriately discounted in view of the occasion of his statement, but there is no reason to reject the thrust of his remarks. The USSR has declared itself to be a global power, and it patently has the capability of acting as one. It may have to withdraw from its forward positions, as it already has on occasion, but any likely regime in Moscow will insist on claiming the prerogatives—and the burdens—of being a superpower. And this means Soviet efforts, and risk-taking, to exert influence on all the

35. Dinerstein, "The Soviet Outlook," pp. 123-24.

36. "The Foreign Policy of the Soviet Union," *Vital Speeches of the Day*, English translation by Novosti Press Agency of Moscow, vol. 34 (August 15, 1968), p. 642. (Emphasis added.)

continents, particularly on the regions of traditionally greatest strategic interest, among which the Middle East occupies a top place.

Western Europe

Virtually every analysis of the postwar political scene puts great stress on the German "problem" in any eventual European political settlement. From the Soviet point of view, this is entirely justified, although it seems to reflect an outmoded view of German power and purpose. Moscow has been concerned with Germany, to the point of obsession, at every stage of its development since 1945. Premier Aleksei Kosygin may have summed up the Soviet attitude best:

I think the major contribution that the Federal Republic of Germany can make to the problem of European security is that it must have a clear and accurate conception of the situation in Europe, where two German states exist—the GDR and the FRG—and no forces from the outside can change this situation. Any other judgments on this score are unrealistic. The second is that the boundaries in Europe that were formed after World War II are inviolable. Moreover, West Germany must renounce forever any claims on nuclear weapons. If the FRG recognizes these circumstances, it will make a great contribution to the cause of easing tensions in Europe and to the cause of ensuring European security.[37]

Since 1966, when Kosygin laid down these dicta, the three Soviet conditions have been met. Even if these were not maximum Soviet aims, as presumably they were not, it would be difficult to argue that nothing has changed in Soviet relations with Western Europe. Either validating the Central European status quo is important to Moscow, or the Soviet Union engaged in a lengthy and intensive diplomatic effort, which ended in success, purely as an exercise. The latter thesis simply is not credible. Tensions in Europe have been further relaxed, and we must assume that this is in accord with Moscow's desires.

There are in fact important reasons—the conflict with Communist China, domestic economic troubles—why the USSR should be interested in European détente based on the newly defined status quo. The difficulty is that the status quo inevitably will come under pressure, mainly from within the Eastern bloc itself. And, aside from everything else, the pragmatic politicians who run the Soviet Union cannot afford to relax completely in their attitudes toward Western Europe.

The Soviet leaders must be aware that a divided Germany is only a little less artificial after the Soviet-German treaty than it was before. The GDR will

37. *Pravda* (Moscow), December 5, 1966.

still need Soviet support, including the presence of Soviet troops. Gromyko seemed to have in mind the fundamental instability of the East German state when he warned the Federal Republic:

Strict observance of the letter and spirit of the treaty is the right way to ensure that the new situation . . . gives rise to genuine confidence and that relations between our countries continually follow the upward trend. The Soviet Union is prepared to follow this way. We certainly expect the Federal Republic of Germany to take a similar approach to the treaty.[38]

But of course the Federal Republic cannot through forbearance create a popular government in East Germany. On the contrary, increased contacts between West and East will contribute inevitably to discontent and potential unrest in East Germany and in other Eastern European nations.

In this situation, the Soviet attitude toward Western Europe will probably continue to be one of vigilance—and occasionally of truculence. If, moreover, the trend toward Western European unification continues, the USSR may be counted on to have its own, unfriendly, view of the process. Even the somewhat remote possibility that a rival power might be established in Europe is bound to be unattractive to the USSR—the one existing superpower on the continent.[39]

Indeed there is no reason to suppose that Soviet goals in Western Europe have changed or will change. Whether we think of the USSR as merely another great power or as the leader of an ideological crusade, the withdrawal of U.S. military power and the acceptance by Europe of the Soviet Union's dominant political role are natural and logical Soviet objectives. It is not necessary, or sensible, to believe that the USSR can accomplish these ends easily or quickly. It is, however, only prudent to assume that Soviet policies will be directed toward them for the indefinite future.

The nonmilitary means and instruments by which the USSR might pursue its aims in Western Europe are not impressive. The communist parties exert

38. Statement to the Presidium of the Supreme Soviet, May 31, 1972. Tass International Service (English ed.; reported in Foreign Broadcast Information Service, *Daily Report: Soviet Union,* May 31, 1972).

39. As Malcolm Mackintosh has said: "The Russians have always felt drawn to the idea that in any geographical grouping of states, the most powerful nation should naturally assume the leadership of the group; therefore, in the most general terms, the Russians feel that Europe is part of their continent, and that they have the right to be predominant in the European area. The presence of any other super-power, under whatever pretext, in Europe is regarded, in this broad sense, as an intrusion, to be eliminated if possible. . . . Soviet aims in Europe are formulated against a background of a long-standing Russian conviction that Europe should rightfully be part of their sphere of interest, just as it is geographically part of the Eurasian continent," "Soviet Aims and Capabilities in Europe," *Royal United Service Institution Journal* (London), March 1971, p. 22.

.

only limited influence. European youth appear to be volatile enough but they do not respond affirmatively to the Soviet message. A deal with West Germany, using the bait of reunification, has receded even further as a possibility— which was never great—given the course of the Federal Republic's Ostpolitik. Pressure on European fuel supplies from the Middle East is a feasible policy for the Arab countries to follow, but there is no reason to believe that they will gear this policy to Soviet objectives.

In the circumstances, Moscow's best prospects appear to lie in the self-induced dissolution of Western political and military relationships, rather than in anything the Soviets might do themselves. If the military predominance of the USSR in Europe could be assured by the withdrawal of American forces— or if the Western European nations and the United States were to part political company decisively—then the Soviets would have a much wider field for applying direct and indirect pressures on Western Europe. Whether Moscow considers this a real possibility for the short run will not be made known to us. There can be little doubt, however, that the essence of Soviet policy toward Western Europe must be to foster whatever disintegrative tendencies may exist or develop, and to act on them when and if the occasion arises.

The United States

Bilateral relations between the Soviet Union and the United States may be said to have been, on the whole, in a warming phase since 1963. In that year, in the wake of the Cuban crisis in 1962, understandings were reached on the Washington-Moscow "hot-line" and the partial nuclear test ban. Thereafter— despite Vietnam, despite the Arab-Israeli hostilities, despite Czechoslovakia, and despite the reams of paper devoted to attacks on U.S. "imperialism"—the relationship has been marked by a continuing search for areas of agreement, by the absence of Soviet threats (notably in Berlin), and by the avoidance of direct military confrontations. A civil aviation accord was reached in 1966, a treaty on the peaceful uses of outer space in 1967, and one prohibiting nuclear weapons on the seabed in 1970. The nonproliferation treaty was signed in 1968; an agreement was reached on measures to reduce the risk of an outbreak of nuclear war between the United States and the USSR in 1971; the SALT I and other agreements were signed at the Moscow summit meeting in 1972; and further progress on SALT II was made at the 1974 Vladivostok summit.

The Basic Principles of Relations, subscribed to on May 29, 1972, by President Nixon and Secretary General Brezhnev, seem to underline a commitment to superpower coexistence as a tenet of Soviet policy. Applied literally, the principles would mean that many old issues would be resolved and that restraint would be practiced virtually on a global basis. "Both sides recognize that efforts to obtain unilateral advantage at the expense of the other, directly or indirectly, are inconsistent with these objectives [of avoiding military confrontations and preventing nuclear war]."[40]

Taken together with the substantive understandings, and particularly with the agreements on the limitation of strategic arms, the principles surely must be seen as a serious expression of the present Soviet attitude toward its relations with the United States. It is possible, to be sure, to construe the Soviet view of détente as being wholly hypocritical. There is a long record that supports this view. But it is not possible to construe the agreements on substantive issues—again with special emphasis on the several accords on armaments—as a kind of Soviet confidence game. Failure to live up to the terms of the agreements would impose costs on the Soviet Union; these costs at some point might appear to the Soviet leaders to be acceptable, and the agreements to be dispensable; but the decision could not be taken casually or lightly. And even the rhetorical commitments, taking account of the context in which they were made, could be openly repudiated in the future only at some expense to the USSR. All in all, it is reasonable to assume that the dominant faction in the Soviet regime would like at this time to pursue in practice the publicly espoused policy—that is, to conduct its relations with the United States in a prudent and restrained manner.

Behind current Soviet viewpoints, moreover, are several compelling considerations: the troubled relations with China, the domestic economic problem, the perception that a nuclear conflict would be a catastrophe for the USSR as well as for the United States, and, not least important, satisfaction at having been publicly recognized as the other world power. It is highly plausible that to the Soviets the objective situation, to use a familiar communist catch-phrase, calls for a continuing interval of respite from excessive Soviet-American tension.

How long the current phase will last is not predictable. Some reservations are in order. One has to do with the dynamics of the Soviet system. Will it be feasible to maintain political control in the Soviet Union without an external focus of hostility? If, as Michel Tatu suggests, "the 'need for enemies' is a fundamental element in the philosophy of the Soviet system,"[41] détente with

40. "Basic Principles of Relations between the United States of America and the Union of Soviet Socialist Republics," *Weekly Compilation of Presidential Documents,* vol. 8 (June 5, 1972), pp. 943-44.

41. Michel Tatu, "The East: Détente and Confrontation," in *Europe and America in the 1970s: I. Between Détente and Confrontation,* Adelphi Papers, 70 (London: Institute for Strategic Studies, 1970), p. 21.

the United States may not be a tenable policy for long.[42] In the ongoing struggle for power within the Kremlin, any faction devoted to peaceful coexistence with the United States must sooner or later face the problem of maintaining its ideological basis of power. Without the imperialist threat to rally them, can the party cadres be counted upon to be reliable? A government that constantly demands great sacrifices from its constituents, and that in any case has a tenuous claim to legitimacy, might well find it necessary to resurrect or reinvent an enemy.

A second reservation is the perennial question concerning the Eastern European countries. As has been demonstrated in the past, these countries are eager to seize opportunities to become more independent of Moscow. The Soviet-Chinese schism made it safe for Romania to opt for a nationalist policy, and the West German Ostpolitik probably encouraged the Czechs in their ill-fated experiment with reform and autonomy.[43] In an era of Soviet-American rapprochement, the Eastern Europeans cannot fail to seek more contacts with the West and greater freedom from Soviet mastery. How far this will be allowed to go, and whether it will be a snowballing process that threatens Moscow's control, are questions that bear directly on the durability of Soviet policy toward the United States.

The Middle East presents further uncertainties. Soviet concern for détente with the United States has not deterred Moscow from arming and rearming Egypt and Syria. In 1956, in 1967, and again in 1973, Arab-Israeli hostilities have led the USSR to issue grave official warnings that it considered Soviet interests to be involved. What a renewed Near Eastern war could bring in its train is an unpredictable but deeply disturbing element in the great power relationship.

Finally, there is the remote possibility of a Sino-Soviet accommodation. Both in China and the USSR new leaders will take over within a few years, and a settlement of the major issues might be in their interest. In that case (which must, however, be considered unlikely), a resumption of the cold war with the West could well follow.

At this stage, it is enough to note these questions about future Soviet policy. Even in its present phase, moreover, Soviet—no less than U.S.—leaders set limits to détente. It is evident that they will bargain hard in arms control negotiations and refuse to sign any agreement that they believe would create

---

42. See also Marshall Shulman, "Political Problems for Both Sides," *Washington Post,* June 4, 1972.

43. Ulam, *Expansion and Coexistence,* pp. 712-13; see also Tatu, *The Great Power Triangle.*

a situation less advantageous for the USSR than the one that would exist in its absence. Their recent actions in the Middle East make it clear that they have no intention of abandoning important goals or allies in order to accommodate the requirements of détente, even if this brings them into limited political collision with the United States. They presumably will not, however, knowingly risk war except to maintain control over their own country and its Eastern European neighbors. Their global policy will thus continue to combine cooperation and competition, with the balance between the two depending on circumstances that vary from region to region. With this mixed and uncertain background we turn to problems of Atlantic defense.

CHAPTER FOUR

WESTERN EUROPE

The reactions of European countries to the October 1973 war in the Middle East and the resulting energy crisis raised the question—which no examination of Atlantic prospects can ignore—whether the movement toward greater Western European unity is petering out. For two decades the trend in Western Europe has been, slowly and erratically, toward integration of the individual nations into a regional grouping. The forces behind this have in the past been strong enough to overcome or to wait out a series of obstacles and interruptions. The proclaimed objective of monetary and economic union in Western Europe by 1980 is rhetorical rather than realistic; but European leaders continue to say that during the 1970s the members of the Community will go considerably farther in the direction of common actions and policies, even though individual countries may retain many of the attributes of sovereign states. Will this actually happen?

One way to assess Europe's future would be to examine the other possibilities. The logical alternatives to gradual and partial integration in Europe are early federation and unification, on the one hand, or stagnation and disintegration of the regional movement on the other.

Federation Now

It is possible that enough of a shock from the outside, which could result only from actions on the part of the United States or the Soviet Union, would move Western Europe within this decade to full unification—political, military, economic, and social. A relapse of the United States into isolationism might provide such a shock, as also might an unmistakable threat of Soviet military aggression. These are imponderables, however. In the normal course of events, popular attachment to the nation state and the formidable problems of achieving basic political change would work against European federation, for the 1970s at least.

33

On this score, while the supposed British capacity for achieving compromise could help the process of regional integration and coordination, Britain in the Community will work against political unification. Taking into account the fact that accession itself was a hard-fought issue, any government in London will certainly be cautious about delegating an important part of its national authority to a supranational body. What applies in Britain also does in France and in varying degrees elsewhere; concern for national autonomy, both real and imagined, is still a powerful factor in European life.

That the European Community has brought into "association" with it the neutral countries of Europe, as well as others, is likely to complicate the situation further. The problem of accommodating the national views of nine countries will be formidable; on some issues, in due course, the number will be sixteen or, with Spain, seventeen. But the fundamental obstacle to unification is not the number of countries involved but rather their persistent attachment to their own national interests, even national interest narrowly conceived.

The case of defense may be considered as a key indicator of the prospects for European unification.[1] From the time of the debate over a European Defence Community (EDC), the idea of specifically European cooperation in defense has had considerable appeal because of: (1) concern about the durability of the American security commitment to Europe; (2) unhappiness over the dominant U.S. role in NATO; (3) hope that joint defense projects could stimulate European technological and industrial advance (especially in relation to the United States); (4) hope that collaboration in defense would hasten political union; and (5) realization that to become a political entity Europe obviously must have a European defense establishment.[2] The important point is that so little has come from these arguments.

European cooperation in arms procurement and in logistics would seem to be an especially promising area for joint action. Nevertheless, accomplishments have been meager and the record discouraging. Deciding what arms are needed, and apportioning them and their production and costs among participating countries, have proved to be extraordinarily difficult problems. In practice no European nation has been ready to make the hard political decisions necessary to overcome local, sometimes exceedingly parochial, interests. Integrated logistics systems have raised similarly difficult questions related to operational

1. A more detailed analysis of prospects in this field is given in chapter 5.
2. "Can one conceive, over the long term, of a Europe growing together . . . in an increasing number of ways and yet not trying to provide coherently for its own defence? I do not myself think it realistic. . . ." Edward Heath, *Old World, New Horizons: Britain, the Common Market, and the Atlantic Alliance* (London: Oxford University Press, 1970), p. 72.

control, procurement, and finance.[3] (Within the larger NATO framework, efforts to promote integrated logistics arrangements have also, in general, had equally limited results, and for similar reasons.)

The Eurogroup, which consists of ten of the European NATO members, can be seen as a tentative step toward reviving the idea of a European defense organization.[4] It was wisely begun with efforts to coordinate European views in NATO and to reexamine questions of common services and doctrine and is far from seeking to create a European military community from the top down. And the perennial thought that British and French nuclear capabilities might be brought together into a specifically European nuclear deterrent force has remained just that—a perennial thought.

In the defense sector, in short, the European idea has had only a limited impact on actual developments. This could change, and some observers believe it will. But the experience of the recent past strongly reinforces the conclusions presented in chapter 5, that very sizable, and for the present insuperable, obstacles will continue to hamper progress toward anything like a genuinely European defense and therefore toward full European unification.

The basic problem in both the monetary and defense fields is the unwillingness of national political leaders and electorates to relax their grip on decisions that they can more readily control on a national than on an international basis. Neither leaders nor voters are willing to surrender that control to a multinational process whose nature and outcome can be only dimly foreseen. This will not soon change.

Disintegration

If early unification looks improbable, what about the abandonment of the European idea altogether? This outcome seems about as unlikely a development as instant unification. For one thing, it would run counter to public attitudes in the continental countries that are members of the European Community. The preponderant evidence from public opinion surveys is that the

3. See Walter Schutze, "European Defense Cooperation—NATO," *The Atlantic Papers,* No. 3 (Paris: The Atlantic Institute, 1969); also Geoffrey Ashcroft, *Military Logistics Systems in NATO: The Goal of Integration,* Pts. 1 and 2, Adelphi Papers, 62 and 69 (London: Institute of Strategic Studies, 1969 and 1970); also Robert Rhodes James, *Standardization and Common Production of Weapons in NATO,* Studies in Defence, Technology, and the Western Alliance, No. 3 (London: Institute of Strategic Studies, 1967).

4. Eurogroup, formed in November 1968 at Brussels, is composed of the defense ministers of Belgium, Denmark, the Federal Republic of Germany, Greece, Italy, Luxembourg, the Netherlands, Norway, Turkey, and the United Kingdom.

goal of "European unity" is widely accepted.[5] In France, where General de Gaulle gave strong and articulate expression over a period of several years to the view that real integration should be resisted, support in French opinion polls for "efforts toward European unification" rose steadily throughout his years of power and reached almost 80 percent by 1970. Entry of the United Kingdom into the Community was clearly favored by the majority in the six original member countries. Interestingly, in light of the current emphasis on the attitude of youth, the 16-to-24 age group, on the continent and in the United Kingdom alike, has been the most favorable to the Community and its expansion.

In some countries, a commitment to the integration of Europe is of long standing and may be considered to be almost a constant in political life. German leadership, for instance, has consistently pursued integration in order to reestablish its national respectability and strengthen its security. It is now perceived as an essential Western anchor to Germany's Eastern policy. In Italy, noncommunist politicians from the earliest postwar years have seen in some form of European organization the route to participation by Italy in world affairs and a source of political strength at home; and the Italian experience within the European Community has confirmed that the European idea also has important economic benefits. The attachment of the Netherlands to a larger Europe grew out of the shock that war and occupation visited on the Dutch. Much the same may be said of Belgium.

These relatively enduring sentiments could not overcome General de Gaulle's differing vision during the 1963-69 period. Since any idea of a larger Europe without France would have been a manifest absurdity, the Community had little choice but to mark time during these years. President Pompidou tried on occasion to emulate the general's attitudes, but without his rhetoric. He succeeded in further dividing and paralyzing Europe by suggesting that unity could be achieved only on French terms; the other Community members accepted inaction and face-saving compromises, but not his vision of the future. Giscard d'Estaing evidently has a somewhat more positive view than his two predecessors, although he remains skeptical of supranationalism.

However, events demonstrated the relative impotence of a middle power—even one guided by so gifted a statesman as General de Gaulle—in a superpower world, and this lesson has not been lost on European political leaders. The realization that none of the Western European states can aspire to major

5. See Ronald Inglehart, "Changing Value Priorities and European Integration," *Journal of Common Market Studies*, vol. 10 (September 1971), pp. 29ff. Also Richard L. Merritt and Donald J. Puchala, *Western European Perspectives on International Affairs: Public Opinion Studies and Evaluations* (Praeger, 1968).

influence in European, to say nothing of global, political and military affairs provides a continuing reason for even Labour leaders in the United Kingdom and the post-Pompidou leadership in France to join with those of Germany and Italy in seeking bases for common European policies. And if the dialogue between the United States and the USSR proves to be continuing and close, it will underscore the limited relevance to important world issues of the view of any one European nation. This will not assure early unification, but it will help to inhibit actions that might destroy the progress already achieved.

It is not just that European politicians are uncomfortable about the minor role allotted to their countries. Intellectuals—many of whom resent what they see as the commanding military, political, and technological position of the United States—and others concerned about Western Europe's military weakness compared with the Soviet Union promote Europeanism in the press and in other opinion media and provide theoretical ballast to policymakers. Businessmen who worry about U.S. competition see hope in the development of European enterprises. These attitudes provide support for the European idea. There is no great likelihood that they will lose their appeal or their strength, even if they are not very easily translated into action.

Above all, European integration to date has been a successful venture economically. The limited European Community has been associated with high employment and rising incomes, and it is doubtful that many Europeans would want to risk losing the advantages, large and small, that seem inherent in the Community idea.

The integration process has been proceeding quietly in Europe. Spain has been associated with the Community since 1970 under a preferential trade arrangement. If a more liberal regime eventually takes over in Madrid, the links with Spain doubtless will be tightened. The neutral countries—Sweden, Switzerland, Austria, and Finland—as well as Norway, Portugal, and Iceland—have come into the Community's commercial orbit, so that a modified free trade area covering all of Europe is a long way toward being a reality. Sweden is associated with Germany, Benelux, and Denmark in the common management of exchange rates. While no dramatic political developments will arise from these economic arrangements, a Europe without customs barriers and with a minimum of border formalities will be very different from the one that existed before the war.

Gradualism

Thus neither early political union nor fragmentation seems likely in Western Europe. Rather, what might be called gradually developing Europeanism, in the economic and also the political and military areas, looks most likely for the years just ahead. It turns out apparently that certain forms of nationalism and the idea of a European personality are not inconsistent. Today a citizen of France, for example, can be at once a "European" to the rest of the world and a loyal Frenchman within his own nation.[6] A gradually "integrating" Europe can be seen in broad outline even now.

Economic Features

In the commercial area, free trade in industrial goods will probably in a few years extend throughout all of Western Europe. Special trade arrangements are in being with nonmember countries in Africa and along the rim of the Mediterranean, and with some of the smaller members in the British Commonwealth. The EC countries already account for more than 40 percent of world exports, and Europe's role as the preeminent world trader will in almost any conceivable situation remain beyond challenge.

While the common agricultural policy of the Community is in need of reform to reduce its costs and to make it more relevant to the problems of the poorer farmers and less of an irritant in the Community's international relationships, no member is likely to want a return to the uncoordinated national policies that existed before the common policy was created. The next steps will be toward a modified but still common farm policy.

Already the Community has moved ahead in varying degree with tax harmonization, a European patent system, and a common antimonopoly policy. National sovereignty has been chipped away, in small bits but at a fairly steady rate. It is a process that is bound to continue, since the issues are ones where convenience will be served by common policies and where no overriding problems of supranationalism need arise.

There are also other economic forces that should press Western Europe toward common policies. One is the energy problem, which now looms large. In a quite literal sense, normal economic activity in Europe depends on the answers to this problem. A common energy policy has been under discussion in the Community for several years; although the member states' policy differences have been wide and have widened further in the present crisis, the goal of a joint approach is not likely to be abandoned. The ability of all Western European states except France to agree on a common European policy at the February 1974 energy conference in Washington suggests that this is perceived

6. See Theodore Geiger, *Transatlantic Relations in the Prospect of an Enlarged European Community* (British-North American Committee, 1970), chap. 2.

by at least eight of the nine Community members. The course of further meetings in the summer, fall, and early winter of 1974 confirms this judgment,
and the Martinique agreement holds out hope of French cooperation.

Investment in Western Europe by American firms—the so-called multinational corporations—has grown without any serious check throughout the
postwar years, despite much uneasiness and some outright hostility on the
part of European businessmen, intellectuals, publicists, and political figures.[7]
The obvious benefits flowing from U.S. investments, the intra-European competition for these benefits, and the fact that European firms also invest abroad,
have worked against any effective measures to discourage or control capital
flows from the United States. This issue has broad appeal, however, and it will
be surprising if the enlarged European Community does not pursue measures
to support "European" firms in technologically advanced fields and otherwise seek ways to join together in competing with the American giants.[8]

The most ambitious European objective is monetary and economic union
by 1980. However, in its current form it is also the least likely of accomplishment, for it raises fundamental economic and political issues. In a monetary
union, the members would give up their individual monetary policy instruments for managing their own economies—that is, for determining levels of
employment. Economic union means that they would operate fiscal instruments (tax and budget policies) in a harmonized (or, as the Werner Report[9]
says, "common") fashion. This would represent substantial integration for a
Community that still consists of individual national economies with differing
tendencies toward stability and inflation. Nevertheless, there is strong political
interest in pursuing the goal of economic integration, and various experiments
will undoubtedly be made until—probably at a much later date than is now
projected—a working formula for progress has been found.

7. "The spectre of American technological domination . . . has perhaps done more to
extend the influence of President de Gaulle—in Britain, in Germany, even in Italy—than
any other single factor, except the Vietnam war." Alastair Buchan, *The Implications of a
European System for Defence Technology*, No. 6, *Defence, Technology and the Western
Alliance* (London: Institute for Strategic Studies, 1967), p. 7.

8. The Commission of the European Communities in 1970 prepared an extensive
report on the industrial policy of the Community, which bears on the investment question. See "Common Industrial Policy: Commission Memorandum Draws Outlines," in
European Community, No. 133 (April 1970).

9. *Report to the Council and Commission on the Realisation by Stages of Economic
and Monetary Union in the Community.* Supplement to *Bulletin of the European Communities*, 11-70, the Werner Group, under the chairmanship of Pierre Werner (Luxembourg: Office of the Official Publications of the European Communities, October 8,
1970).

Environmental Cooperation

Threats to the environment will also bring the European states together in formal and organized ways. The pollution of Europe's rivers and lakes has already caused enough alarm to lead to the creation of no fewer than eight interstate commissions. The Council of Europe and the European Community's Commission have competence and interest in carrying out antipollution measures, and their secretariats may be expected to pursue with some persistence this newer field of activity.[10] Since many environmental problems are bilateral or regional in character, the proliferation of remedial organizations is inevitable. But if the issues are as serious and politically compelling as they seem destined to be, pressures will develop to Europeanize the environmental machinery, if only to agree on common standards and principles for achieving economies of scale and for avoiding competitive distortions in trade.

Political Coordination

Many observers have pointed out that creating a customs union and a common agricultural policy will not lead in any automatic way to political unity in Europe.[11] Events have confirmed this. Further economic integration may call for the invention of new—European—political instruments, but it will still leave Europe without a common policy for external affairs, to say nothing of a common European executive and parliament.

The principal current experiment in political cooperation in Europe—the committee of foreign ministers—veers well away from supranationalism toward the coordination of national foreign policies.[12] The "coordination" of national policies may fall short of decisionmaking by a "European" body, but it is not a meaningless exercise either. For some time, at any rate, it will be the preferred method, since the supranational political body—a popularly elected European Parliament—that is needed to guide Europe to unified foreign policies is still far in the future.

One may question, moreover, whether a distinctive European role in most affairs outside the continent will have so strong an attraction. Not only are

10. Jon McLin, *European Organizations and the Environment,* Fieldstaff Reports, West Europe Series, vol. 7, no. 2 (American Universities Field Staff and California Institute of Technology, 1972).

11. See Raymond Aron, *Peace and War: A Theory of International Relations,* English translation by Richard Howard and Annette Baker Fox (Doubleday, 1966), pp. 746-49.

12. It is a return to the coordinating committee concept underlying France's Fouchet Plan of 1961, which then was (and still is) compatible with the British view of practicalities. See Miriam Camps, *European Unification in the Sixties* (McGraw-Hill, 1966), p. 126. See also Heath, *Old World, New Horizons,* pp. 53-58.

the principal European powers reluctant to contemplate incurring the costs of activist external policies, but even a slowly integrating Western Europe will tend to be preoccupied with its own internal problems, which are extremely demanding on the time and energies of officials and politicians. In these circumstances, already-existing machinery for discussing and coordinating the various national foreign policy views probably will seem adequate to the needs of the 1970s.

Where a Western European foreign policy would be of great importance, of course, is in the relationships with the Soviet Union and Eastern Europe. Here, if anywhere, the pressure will be for agreed positions among the major Western European nations, since some form of ongoing multilateral discussion with Eastern Europe seems all but certain. If there are serious differences among the policies of France, Germany, and Great Britain, the possibility that Western Europe will influence the superpowers in these exchanges will be very much diminished; and the USSR will have been given, at no cost, opportunities to influence developments in Western Europe.

An Integrating Europe and the Atlantic Connection

The prospect then is that on the European side of the Atlantic connection at least into the 1980s there will still be a group of national states that are working toward, and to some extent preoccupied with, the objective of European integration. It will not be the Europe of the two-pillar theory—a united Europe to match the United States—but its members will in some degree be acting in concert on European matters and seeking to present a common policy front to other parts of the world.

Such a Europe will not easily find a harmonious relationship with the United States and Canada. It is already an old American complaint that the countries of the Community have been excessively absorbed in their regional problems, looking "inward" rather than "outward" and acting in a parochial rather than in a "responsible" manner. It is likely that the larger European group that is envisaged, wrestling with increasingly complex problems, will continue to show these characteristics.

As the integration process continues, moreover, European domestic politics will be devoted in considerable measure to integration issues. There will be many opportunities to find partisan ammunition in the economic and political problems that are bound to bedevil an integrating Europe. And it is only realistic to expect that the United States will continue to find itself a target for attack as being hostile to particular European interests or responsible for European difficulties.

It could scarcely be otherwise with the transatlantic relationships so numerous and close and the American presence in Europe so ubiquitous. There are vocal sectors of European opinion, extending across the political spectrum in all countries, where dislike or distrust of the United States is endemic. And there are differences not only of culture but of substance, especially in economic relations, that will provide reasons for Europe to resist American "pressures." To these issues of substance we now turn, beginning with the area where there has traditionally been the greatest common interest—defense.

CHAPTER FIVE

MAINTAINING THE COMMON DEFENSE

Total Soviet conventional military power will continue to exceed that of the Western European states for the foreseeable future. This, of course, does not mean that the Soviets are superior in manpower or resources. On both scores, Western Europe has the greater capabilities. It is mainly the consequence of a political choice among priorities, which in the Soviet Union is made quite readily in favor of armed strength, while in Western Europe military spending is subject to much tighter political constraints. Because of the constraints, the presence of sizable U.S. conventional military forces in Europe is an important element in the current balance of nonnuclear military power on the continent, and this is likely to continue for at least the rest of the 1970s.

Opinions differ widely about the comparative military strength in Europe of the Warsaw Pact countries and NATO and depend to a considerable extent on qualitative judgments about the two sides. In any case, in the central region, where the principal ground forces confront one another, the NATO armies have about 365,000 ground combat troops deployed against 355,000 Soviet soldiers and perhaps 145,000 from other Warsaw Pact countries.[1] The Soviets have a numerical advantage in tanks, which is offset by what is generally considered to be NATO's qualitative advantage in tactical airpower. The 90,000 U.S. combat soldiers make up about one-fourth of the NATO total; and the United States provides about one-fourth of NATO's tank forces and one-third of its tactical aircraft.[2] Without the U.S. contribution no successful conventional defense of Western Europe would be possible.

The character and credibility of the U.S. nuclear commitment to Europe also depends on the deployment of these U.S. troops in Europe. Undoubtedly

1. Charles L. Schultze and others, *Setting National Priorities: The 1974 Budget* (Brookings Institution, 1973), pp. 354-55. The "other Warsaw Pact" forces are considered to be those that are prospectively available for offensive use.
2. Ibid., p. 358.

the American strategic deterrent has lost some of its credibility with allies and potential enemies alike. Any certainty that an American president would call for a nuclear response to aggression in Europe has long since ceased to exist, if indeed it ever existed; and yet a lingering uncertainty about the use of the nuclear weapon—which is the deterrent—will continue at least as long as an American second-strike capability remains. Precisely because the United States, by reason of its military presence in Europe, is intimately involved in developing and carrying out NATO strategy and policy, that uncertainty is magnified.[3] There is no question but that the United States would be engaged in any large East-West war in Europe; and it must be recognized that such an engagement *could* lead to the use of nuclear weapons. If, on the other hand, the United States were not so involved—if, say, American military power were withdrawn from Europe and from European strategic planning—automatic engagement would have ended, and the relevance of the nuclear deterrent would be further and significantly diminished.

Opinions differ as to whether, given the apparently remote possibility of Soviet aggression, a balance of conventional military power must be maintained that reinforces and is reinforced by U.S. nuclear guarantees, in order to avoid hostilities in Europe. However one judges this need, it is clear that promising political and economic trends are also at stake. West Germany is convinced that maintaining a military balance is essential to the effective pursuit of Ostpolitik. Other Western European countries have suggested that U.S. forces are needed to balance German military strength and thus avert the revival of intra-European tensions, which could occur if Germany again became the strongest military power on the continent. And a drastic weakening of the U.S. military presence in Europe could generate transatlantic recrimination that might endanger important cooperative ventures in trade, monetary policy, and aid to developing countries.

Nor could a shift to greater reliance on tactical nuclear weapons mitigate the effects of a cut in U.S. forces. In a military sense, the use of nuclear weapons might well lead to escalation that would destroy the very societies NATO is pledged to defend. In a political sense, a shift to greater reliance on their use would increase—not reduce—the concerns that a unilateral cut in U.S. force levels would cause.

These are crucial considerations that bear on the question why, thirty years after V-day in Europe, large U.S. military forces remain in West Germany. As long as Western Europe's security and economic and political health

3. See Leonard Beaton, *The Strategic and Political Issues Facing America, Britain and Canada* (London: British-North American Committee, 1971), pp. 14-16.

are considered to be vital U.S. interests, the case for an American military presence in Europe cannot readily be rejected.

Yet the difficulties of maintaining the present numbers of troops in Europe are bound to become more pressing. Apart from all else, the underlying reality is that the sharp increases in manpower costs will in time probably lead to further reductions in total U.S. military forces. The political reality, in turn, is that eventually these cuts will have to be made in U.S. forces based in Europe, as well as in those stationed elsewhere—both at home and abroad.

If negotiated mutual force reductions are made, a rough NATO-Warsaw Pact balance will be maintained. But mutual reductions may not be negotiable, at least not before unilateral American force cuts become necessary. So the question is open as to whether NATO's present structure is truly feasible in view of the budget stringencies foreseen in Western Europe and North America. In other words, a rethinking of Western European defense may be unavoidable. What are the possibilities?

European Defense Efforts

An alternative that is attractive to a number of observers would be to phase out direct U.S. military involvement in Europe in favor of a new and eventually wholly European defense structure.[4] The specifics of the proposals vary, but the central theme is that Europe can and should provide increasingly for its own defense, in a continuing but gradually loosening association with the United States. This, it is argued, would comport with an enlarged and integrating European Community, as well as with the uncertainties about the durability of the U.S. military presence in Europe and about the credibility of the U.S. nuclear deterrent.

It is argued in chapter 4 that the limited results of past efforts to move toward a Western European defense system foreshadow only gradual progress at best. Here we look at predictable trends to see whether they are consistent with this prognosis.

An independent military capacity would be within the economic and manpower capabilities of the Western European powers, assuming, of course, that the political will exists to exercise these capabilities as an inevitable concomi-

4. For example, François Duchene, "A New European Defense Community," *Foreign Affairs,* vol. 50 (October 1971), pp. 69-82; Gen. André Beaufré, "Which Strategies for Europe?" (paper prepared for the Committee of Nine, North Atlantic Assembly, 1972, processed by Brookings Institution, Washington, D.C.); and David Calleo, "Alternatives to NATO," in *The Atlantic Fantasy: The U.S., NATO, and Europe* (The Johns Hopkins University Press, 1970), chap. 8.

tant of European integration. But in the near future—that is, into the early 1980s—that will is unlikely to exist. As René Foch has said, in many respects the 1980s are astonishingly near.[5] For Western Europe to be able within this short time to compose its internal differences and make the budgetary and other decisions needed for rapid progress toward a viable separate defense would require a revolution in the European political scene,[6] and there is no evidence that such a revolution is imminent.

The fact that some collective European defense activities are under way suggests, however, that the outlook is not necessarily for immobility. The Eurogroup has strong political support in the United Kingdom and West Germany. European members of NATO's Nuclear Planning Group are conducting their own studies on the concepts of nuclear warfare. The European Defence Improvement Program is the result of serious political consultations. Efforts at multilateral arms production, despite all their disappointments, are not wholly without results. And the lessons of past failures can be drawn upon as economic and political pressures call for more experiments.

Furthermore, external and internal compulsions will work toward cooperation in defense. The Conference on Security and Cooperation in Europe and the negotiation on mutual and balanced force reductions mean that at a minimum an effort must be made to establish Western European positions and policies on major security issues.

As military costs continue to rise, budget stringencies will increasingly impose a need for economy. This need may be met through hitherto untried rationalization measures. Thus a minority recommendation of the Netherlands Commission of Civilian and Military Experts, which was set up to analyze the Dutch defense effort, was that NATO be asked "whether the Netherlands should not . . . relinquish her own air force so as to concentrate effort on the other two armed services. . . ."[7] Such a radical idea is not likely to be accepted soon, but more modest approaches of this kind may be.

What does seem improbable is that a concerted and major effort will be made to build a collective structure that is capable of the independent defense

5. "Europe in 1980" (paper prepared for the Committee of Nine).
6. "The European experiment in unification would have to extend and consolidate itself over several years before it was ready to include defence." Edward Heath, *Old World, New Horizons: Britain, the Common Market, and the Atlantic Alliance* (London: Oxford University Press, 1970), p. 73.
7. Commission of Civilian and Military Experts, "The Future of the Netherlands Defense Effort: Findings and Recommendations," Report to the Government of the Netherlands (March 1972; processed), p. 7.

of Europe. The idea of a European defense centered around the British and French nuclear deterrents is attractive, but its substance is difficult to grasp. This is not to say that the British and French nuclear forces have no deterrent value, for they are another factor making for uncertainty. If they could be combined, this deterrent potential might be enhanced. But as the basis for a European deterrent, the Anglo-French forces are subject to serious question. A European nuclear deterrent would seem to require that West Germany and the rest of Western Europe agree to rely on a guarantee by London and Paris to use nuclear weapons in the event of a Soviet attack in Europe; or that West Germany itself be allowed to determine whether the weapons would be used. Neither of these conditions has the attributes of reality. Thus movement toward Anglo-French nuclear cooperation might well create new political tensions that would inhibit rather than hasten progress toward European unity. For this reason, if for no other, there is no reason for the United States to go out of its way to welcome and assist Anglo-French nuclear accord unless it can be worked out in ways that avoid both discrimination against Germany and the specter of a national German military role. It is doubtful that either of these conditions can be fulfilled without a very high degree of political unification in Western Europe.

Technical questions are probably less difficult, but the costs of creating a genuine second-strike capability surely would be large; the United States has been spending about $18 billion (in 1973 dollars) each year over the past decade to maintain and modernize a strategic nuclear force that had already been built; modernization costs alone over the next ten years are expected to amount to $69 billion.[8] And even if the budgetary and political decisions could be made very soon—an obvious impossibility—and American technical support were forthcoming, it would be well into the 1980s before a European nuclear force with the potential to deliver a second strike could come into being.

A more promising approach might be to integrate the conventional European forces in NATO; in the long run these forces might assume much of the conventional defense burden. This seems technically more feasible than does nuclear integration, but difficult political decisions would have to be made to get it under way. French participation would be essential, but at present is unlikely. Elsewhere, the motivation for making these difficult decisions is not apparent. Perhaps if the United States were to reduce sharply its military presence in Western Europe, a political effort would be made to create a col-

8. Charles L. Schultze and others, *Setting National Priorities: The 1973 Budget* (Brookings Institution, 1972), chap. 3.

lective European system. The obstacles would be great, however, and it seems at least as likely that the European nations would accept the American action passively in the belief that any effort at a European defense would fail.

The prospect thus is that, in the 1970s, on the European defense side of the Atlantic connection, there will still be a group of national European states. Even though its members may be acting more and more in concert on defense matters, the European group will not be mounting a united military effort to match that of the United States. As suggested in chapter 4, gradualism will be the order of the day. If there is progress toward a more concerted European military effort, it is less likely to come about because of a single striking development than to evolve gradually as a result of growing concert among the European countries in planning and procurement. The United States can encourage this trend by making clear that it would welcome the greater European role—even though this involved some decline in U.S. influence and perhaps even in U.S. arms sales to Europe. The objective of U.S. participation in NATO is not to maximize U.S. influence or even U.S. military exports, but to defend Europe; NATO will be a more effective instrument for this purpose if it rests on a more solid European contribution.

Whatever may happen to cooperation on European defense, however, a marked expansion of European ground strength does not appear to be in sight. Except for the United Kingdom, whose volunteer army is as large as it is likely to get and which has no real possibility of reintroducing conscription, the question is not so much one of adequate manpower as of budgets. In theory, both Germany and France draft virtually all physically fit men of military age, thus achieving equity in conscription. But the proportion of eligible men who are actually drafted varies; the periods of training in the use of modern weapons are short; and Germany has lowered its conscription period to fifteen months and France to twelve months. The maneuver forces—which would have to absorb the shock of any conflict while reserves were being mobilized, armed, and further trained—are held within the limits set by relatively fixed budgets.[9] While it would certainly be possible to raise budgetary ceilings sharply enough to increase the numbers of fully equipped, mobile, readily available European forces, the likelihood of such action being taken is very small. Instead, the probable result of present trends will be either actually to

9. Press and Information Office of the German Federal Government, *White Paper, 1973/1974: The Security of the Federal Republic of Germany and the Development of the Federal Armed Forces* (Federal Minister of Defense on behalf of the German Federal Government), 1974, pp. 212ff.

abandon conscription or to build large reserve forces by allowing most drafted men to discharge their military obligations largely through intermittent service in the reserves, rather than through prolonged full-time service in the maneuver forces.

Nor is the prospect any more promising at sea: European naval forces would not be able to replace the U.S. Sixth Fleet in the Mediterranean in the rather unlikely event that Washington decided to withdraw it. The various European fleets in the Mediterranean are not small—either in numbers or in capabilities—but they complement rather than overlap the two aircraft carrier task forces of the Sixth Fleet.[10] Basically, the European naval capability is that of protecting merchant shipping, whereas the U.S. fleet is an attack force. Neither could readily assume the role of the other.

A New Look at NATO

If the "European" option is not truly available, at least in the 1970s, and if the U.S. role in Europe may have to be reduced (and if, to be realistic, European defense budgets in real terms are likely to move downward as other budgetary claims receive priority), what might be done to sustain for a further period an Atlantic defense of Western Europe that would be enough to meet the political needs cited earlier and to discourage, or contain, any East-West hostilities short of a potentially disastrous nuclear exchange?

Although a variety of scenarios can be drawn up for a future European conflict, both East and West have considered Germany to be the central region, figuratively as well as geographically, and have deployed their main ground forces accordingly. Whether it is assumed that war will come by accident—a spillover from upheavals in Eastern Europe—or otherwise, this sector has been the focus of strategic attention. There, as we have seen, the opposing forces are not greatly out of balance—particularly if it is judged that the assumed aggressor, the Warsaw Pact, would need a substantial superiority in combat strength to overrun NATO defenses. This is the more true since some Western analysts believe that NATO's superiority in weaponry and firepower offsets the Soviet advantages. This East-West balance is, to be sure, hypothetical. It could be proved only in practice. And whether it is so or not, substantial U.S. combat forces, whose continued presence in Europe is uncertain, would be an important element in that balance.

10. Arnold M. Kuzmack and Leslie Gelb, "The Balance of Naval Forces in the Mediterranean" (paper prepared for the Committee of Nine).

Soviet strategic planning for the central region appears to be founded on the proposition that a war in Western Europe must be won quickly if it is to be won at all. This is the reason for the emphasis on numbers of tanks, on close tactical air support for ground troops, on a high ratio of combat to support forces, and on logistic capabilities suited to a short conflict of weeks or months, not years. The Soviet strategy, in sum, appears to envision a sharp, decisive thrust that would sweep through the Western European defenses before the greater mobilization capabilities of NATO could be brought to bear. U.S. forces, by contrast, appear geared to a repeat of World War II. Their high ratio of support forces and deep interdiction air forces would be very useful in a prolonged conflict, but would detract from battlefield strength in a short war.

This asymmetry creates both a need and an opportunity. The need is to restructure and redeploy NATO armies in the center to counter Soviet short-war strategy.[11] The opportunity that is created is to reduce the scale and cost of U.S. forces in the process. To meet the need and take advantage of the opportunity, NATO should reexamine fundamentally its planning, logistics, and deployment insofar as they are based on the World War II model. The objective should be to establish a new defense pattern, emphasizing immediate firepower, greatly reduced support and long-lead reserve forces, strengthened logistics for a short conflict, and quick deployment of combat units. On this basis, some manpower and budgetary economies should be possible without sacrificing the defensive strength necessary for the ultimate mission of checking a full-scale Warsaw Pact offensive.

To adapt to the short-war concept, the United States should place heavier reliance on European logistics. This would lead to renewed consideration of more closely integrated supply arrangements within NATO. In fact, quite aside from any review of NATO strategy, the reasons for greater military integration within the alliance are more powerful now than ever. It is a commentary of sorts that after twenty-three years of effort toward a collective defense, NATO logistics remain the responsibility of individual nations. A multinational logistics system supporting NATO forces on the central front would be justified because of its greater efficiency and reliability in case of war. Present U.S. logistic operating expenditures in Europe could eventually be reduced as a result. The constraints on national military budgets in the NATO countries are well known and understandable, although they result to some degree in an inequitable sharing of burdens. Less defensible has been the universal

11. Richard D. Lawrence and Jeffrey Record, *U.S. Force Structure in NATO: An Alternative* (Brookings Institution, 1974).

inability of NATO members to override parochial interests in favor of common actions in such areas as logistics—actions that could, among other benefits, save on military budgets.[12]

A NATO common market in defense products is no doubt unrealistic on a large scale in view of the tenacity with which each country clings to its domestic armaments industry. Nevertheless, there should be possibilities—and budgetary pressures—for more efficient military procurement in the NATO area. Measures that allow greater freedom in military procurement give rise to the same welfare benefits as those that are gained from greater freedom of trade in nonmilitary goods. In the military, as in the economic, sphere, the first movement in this direction may be made by the European countries cooperating among themselves. As in the economic area, some discrimination against U.S. exports may be an inevitable, if temporary, result. This discrimination should be accepted as it was in the economic field when the Common Market was first formed—because of the larger benefits for European unity. And it is not clear that European cooperation in production and procurement, if it focused on areas where Europe has potentially the largest comparative advantage, would work to any great extent against rational allocation of production and procurement among the Atlantic countries.

The argument in favor of greater integration of equipment and logistics in NATO—whether on a European or an Atlantic basis—is not only that it would be more efficient, but that it would demonstrate the cohesion and resolve of the alliance. As a show of NATO unity and renewal, it would impress the Soviet Union as much as ten years' supply of ministerial resolutions. And in a period when manpower levels—in other than territorial forces at least—will be static or declining, the visible strengthening of NATO as an alliance could not be considered by the Warsaw Pact to be provocative or disruptive of détente.

But more important than rationalizing production and procurement would be to revise NATO's military structure along the lines suggested earlier. These changes must be made multilaterally if they are to be effective, and this will take time. Political decisions will need to be made, and the process of carrying out the decisions will be lengthy. Fortunately, the time is likely to be available. The negotiations on mutual force reductions may work to defer immediate pressures from Congress to take U.S. troops out of Europe; and

12. Harlan Cleveland, *NATO: The Transatlantic Bargain* (Harper and Row, 1970), pp. 86–91. René Foch in his paper for the Committee of Nine comments that since the beginning of the Common Market the price of refrigerators has dropped by more than half, while the price of a tank has doubled; he attributes this to the "absurdity" of having a division of labor in consumer goods but not in military equipment.

the more basic issue of the manpower squeeze on U.S. military forces is a longer-term matter. Meanwhile the critical need is to get on with a restructuring of NATO forces. If anything can be said with assurance, it is that events will overtake a standpat military position in Western Europe, to the potential detriment of a believable security system.

Burden-Sharing

One of the long-standing contentious issues within NATO has been who should bear the "costs" of the U.S. (and British) forces stationed in Western Europe. Typically, the question has been complicated by a confusion between the concept of real costs in resources and the idea of a balance-of-payments "burden" associated with stationing troops abroad.

Wherever servicemen are located, of course, their pay and allowances must continue. Only demobilization would eliminate these budgetary expenditures. The added real costs for overseas troops are the expenses involved in moving men and their families as tours of duty begin and end and the higher transport and storage costs for supplies and equipment; and in recent years the depreciation of the dollar has made it more expensive than before to deploy U.S. soldiers in Europe. Even so, the central issue, as far as resource costs are concerned, is the size of U.S. forces, not their location. To the extent that congressional concern has focused on resource cost sharing, it reflects a general feeling that the United States is contributing too large a share of NATO forces and that the European countries should increase their input of men or of money.

Balance-of-payments costs, in contrast to the budgetary costs, represent the *net* foreign exchange expenditures attributable to forces that are away from their own country. Since these expenditures are necessarily priced together, in balance-of-payments accounting, with all other spending for goods, services, and investment, there are conceptual and practical problems involved in separating out military balance-of-payments figures. To minimize these difficulties, the practice has grown up of counting against foreign exchange outlays for foreign-based troops purchases of military equipment, as well as certain negotiated offsets. The residual has then been called the military balance-of-payments "cost" and has been assumed to be reflected in the external deficits of the United States. Congressional concern has centered on this so-called foreign exchange burden at least as much as it has on the real resource costs of keeping troops in Europe.

In the first place, the argument about foreign exchange costs has lost a great deal of its intensity. Given the general trend toward exchange rate flexibility, it has become much less likely that chronic balance-of-payments surpluses or deficits will be a major problem of the future as among and between the industrial countries. Moreover, the sums involved in military payments have been swamped by the enormous increases in international accounts that have come in the wake of high oil prices and the growth of international trade and capital flows. The difficulties of adjustment to the new balance-of-payments situation in the world are only marginally worsened by the problem of military outpayments and in practice this aspect of the burden-sharing question is likely more and more to be forgotten.

On the side of real costs, however, there remains a case in equity and in politics for saying that countries that send forces abroad in the interests of the common defense should not have to bear the extra costs—or, rather, all of the extra costs—of doing so. This is not a matter of European countries paying "occupation" costs, as it has sometimes been described. Instead, it says that the added budgetary burdens that are involved in a mutual defense system ought to be shared among the participants.

In fact, a useful beginning has been made toward sharing the real costs of U.S. forces in Europe. Under U.S.-Federal Republic of Germany (FRG) offset arrangements, West Germany is providing substantial sums for rehabilitating barracks and like purposes—expenditures that otherwise would have required American dollar outlays in Germany.[13] This approach might logically be extended. The European bases used by American forces could be converted into NATO bases under joint occupancy wherever possible. Then the base costs, which are principally for repair and maintenance, could be shared by host and foreign forces according to an agreed formula. NATO already has some jointly used bases and, as noted, there is the precedent of the barracks improvement program in Germany. These arrangements could be applied as standard procedures throughout the NATO region with such local adjustments and exceptions as might be required.

Whether this approach or any variant thereof would be negotiable is not certain. It would require European legislatures to appropriate funds to pay some of the costs of foreign troops—which they have traditionally resisted. On the other hand, the appropriations would go to the alliance and would contribute to its cohesion and effectiveness. If the burden-sharing question

13. See Press and Information Office of the German Federal Government, *White Paper, 1973/1974,* p. 21.

is to be managed in a way that will make for a stronger and more durable
Atlantic defense connection, a plan that will do this needs to be found.

Conclusion

The main issues confronting the alliance in the defense field are political,
not military. At present there is a rough balance of forces in Central Europe,
but that balance is endangered by pressures to reduce NATO—and particularly
U.S.—forces in Europe. In some degree, these pressures are likely to prevail,
and the alliance's task is to adjust its present plans and deployments to this
prospect. The most promising way of doing this unilaterally would be to
move toward the concept of a short (thirty- to sixty-day) war and make the
changes in the NATO—and particularly the U.S.—force structures that this
would entail. It will take time. Negotiations about mutual force reductions,
which are discussed in chapter 6, and which may themselves ease the shift to
lower force levels, are likely to relieve pressures for unilateral reductions sufficiently to gain that time.

Once lower force levels have been achieved, the task will be to stabilize
NATO forces at these levels. Two steps would be useful to this end:

• A movement toward burden-sharing, for example, by converting U.S.
bases in Europe into allied bases, whose operating costs should be shared by
the allies. This should be proposed by the United States.

• Progress toward more effective European defense cooperation, which
would result in a more effective—although probably not larger—European
contribution to NATO. The United States should make clear that it would
welcome this progress and would be prepared to adjust its role in NATO
accordingly, even if this meant a decline in U.S. influence and military sales
in Europe.

These changes—to a short-war concept, greater burden-sharing, and more
effective cooperation in Western European defense—will each involve difficulties. But the alternative—staying where we are now—is not feasible. The
question is not *whether* to change, but how, and how soon.

CHAPTER SIX

EAST-WEST NEGOTIATIONS

Prospects for European defense depend in part on the outcome of on-going East-West negotiations. The year 1973 marked a new stage in the long post-war confrontation between Eastern Europe and the North Atlantic nations. For the first time, the two groups of countries agreed to negotiate en bloc on matters relating to the future of Europe as a whole. One negotiation, the Conference on Security and Cooperation in Europe (CSCE), includes all of the European states (except Albania), as well as the United States and Canada. The other, on the reduction of military forces in Europe, includes the seven members of the Warsaw Pact and twelve of the fourteen members of NATO (all except Portugal and Iceland). Taken together, these negotiations could bring early and important changes in Europe's political and military relation-ships. Probably, however, the first rounds at least will be neither great suc-cesses nor obvious failures. Rather they will result in some modest agreements that will be accepted as representing further but unspectacular progress toward European détente.

Conference on Security and Cooperation in Europe

Looking first at the CSCE, which inevitably though inaccurately is com-pared with the Congress of Vienna, the most surprising point is that the Western powers should have viewed it with any apprehension. True, when the Soviets first broached the idea of a European security conference, it had every earmark of a rather clumsy attempt to separate Western Europe from the United States and Canada and, within Europe, to isolate West Germany on the issue of two Germanies. On these grounds, the West balked at the pro-posal. But U.S. and Canadian participation was conceded, and the German question in due course was negotiated separately with the Federal Republic of Germany (FRG). By that time, the USSR may have lost interest in the

CSCE. The Eastern European states had not, however, and Moscow may have decided that to abandon the idea would be needlessly annoying to its neighbors and that, in any case, the thirty-four-nation gathering could do no serious harm to Soviet interests. How it could do much harm to Western interests is not clear either.

A major concern was that the conference might foster public complacency about a declining Soviet threat to Western security. Of course, complacency may in some sense be a result of the conference. However, to give weight to this point, it must be assumed that the CSCE will do a great deal more than prepare and agree upon a number of wordy and general resolutions. What could be accomplished that would add much to, say, the impact on public opinion of the Soviet-Polish-West German treaties or the Nixon-Brezhnev summits is not easily foreseen. Anxiety about Soviet intentions has declined as some of the causes of East-West tension have diminished. The CSCE is likely to hasten this process in only marginal ways.

It was also feared that the CSCE would tend to ratify the existing territorial and political situation in Central and Eastern Europe—that is, two Germanies, the Oder-Neisse line as Poland's frontier, and Soviet preeminence over its Eastern European allies. But all these are realities, and there is no disposition in the West to quarrel with them. The CSCE, except perhaps as it brings out the simmering dissidence among the Eastern Europeans, can have very little to do with the current political and territorial situation.

A major item on the CSCE working agenda is "cooperation in the fields of economics, of science and technology and of the environment." The USSR has clearly shown an interest in a further expansion of foreign economic relations. The Lend-Lease settlement with the United States and the emphasis placed by Moscow on most-favored-nation tariff treatment, for example, are ample evidence of this. Undoubtedly the CSCE is viewed as a forum where this policy line can be expounded. It is not at all likely, however, that anything substantial will happen there to make for easier Soviet access to Western technology or credits or markets.

Western technology already is available to the Eastern bloc without any serious restriction. The remaining international controls on so-called strategic goods are extremely limited in scope. And Western Europe and Japan have long been selling virtually all types of industrial equipment freely to the East; three-fourths of Western exports to the East in normal years are of manufactured goods.[1] Long-term credits at favorable interest rates have been readily

1. General Agreement on Tariffs and Trade, *International Trade 1970* (GATT, 1971), Table 10, pp. 22-23.

granted or guaranteed by governments for major industrial items. Despite import barriers in the United States and Western Europe against Eastern European goods, trade between West and East certainly has not stagnated. During the 1960s it grew faster than world trade as a whole; exports to Western countries from Eastern Europe (including the USSR) were more than $18 billion in 1973, compared with about $2 billion in 1960.[2]

The Eastern European countries would like to have greater access to Western markets, including most-favored-nation tariff treatment in the United States, less stringent agricultural trade restrictions in the European Community, and more and easier credits. The USSR might be interested in large intergovernmental loans, on preferential terms, especially in view of its heavy outlays for wheat and feed grain imports in 1972-73. Moscow certainly has an interest in securing financing for natural resource development projects in Siberia. However, these are not matters that could have been negotiated in the CSCE. Substantive agreements, if any, are likely to be on peripheral matters.

For the rest, the working phase of the CSCE in Geneva[3] took up questions relating to security in Europe, cooperation in humanitarian and other fields, and the "follow-up" of the CSCE. The various committees and subcommittees sought to recommend positive action to strengthen confidence and increase stability and security or to facilitate freer East-West movements and contacts. If even modest steps are taken as a result, the conference could be considered a success from a Western point of view. But anyone who hopes for major developments, particularly concerning freedom of movement and information, is almost certain to be disappointed, for the elements of a bargain are lacking. The USSR and most Eastern European governments have little to gain from a larger flow of communications from the West—rather the contrary. And Western tourism in the East will continue to expand without any reciprocal movement from East to West.

That the CSCE should create a permanent body for security and cooperation in Europe has been proposed by Soviet Foreign Minister Andrei Gromyko. If anything in the CSCE could divide the West, it would be to establish such a continuing committee without the United States and Canada being represented. So desirable an outcome from the Soviet point of view is surely out of the question, however; and it is not even clear that the Soviet Union will pursue the idea of an exclusively European security body.

As this is written, it is not clear whether the conference will end with the grand conclave of heads of government desired by the Soviet Union. This

2. U.S. Department of Commerce, unpublished data.
3. The first plenary and speech-making session was held in Helsinki in July 1973.

should now be a matter of the most marginal significance to the Atlantic powers. Such an assemblage of senior politicians could not possibly agree on anything other than a round of vacuous statements having not the slightest prospect of altering the course of events. If it comes to pass, because Mr. Brezhnev's insistence manages to enlist enough Western supporters, the occasion ought to be treated for what it will be, an essentially meaningless formality.

Mutual Reduction of Forces

In contrast to the broad sweep of the CSCE, the East-West discussion on reducing "forces and armaments" is concentrated on the narrower and more definable subject of the military confrontation in Central Europe. It has been customary to see the negotiation on the mutual reduction of forces in Europe as extremely complex—far more so than the talks on limiting strategic arms.[4] It is also sometimes said that mutual reductions cannot benefit NATO security and more probably will favor the Warsaw Pact's military position, perhaps decisively.[5]

These propositions are not without substance. Although "balance" has been dropped from the official terminology, the objective of "undiminished security" for each party leaves room for infinite theoretical debate. Does this objective require detailed measurements of numbers, the eventual positioning of men, firepower, mobility, or combat effectiveness? If emphasis is placed on offensive weapons, what definitions are pertinent to particular items of equipment? If indigenous forces are to be covered, how should a Czech division be weighed against a West German unit? If it is stationed forces, what allowance, if any, is to be made for the factors of time and distance in reintroducing troops? Tactical nuclear weapons are not to be dealt with in the first stages of the negotiations, but this is a topic of great moment that may eventually have to be considered.[6]

4. "It might seem sensible to limit the participants in these talks (whose complexity compared with SALT will be roughly what Spassky-Fischer chess is to dominoes) to the Central European countries." *The Economist,* vol. 244 (August 12, 1972), p. 16.

5. It is generally agreed that NATO's forces have already reached their "critical minimum"; any further reduction would virtually mean the abandonment of a European defense system. Balanced quantitative reductions would sharply increase the present imbalance in Russia's favor; percentage reductions, while leaving the proportionate relationship intact, would in fact weaken the Western side fatally since the critical minimum has already been reached. (Institute for the Study of Conflict, *European Security and the Soviet Problems* [London: the Institute, January 1972], p. 19).

6. A tradeoff between U.S. forward-based nuclear armed aircraft and Soviet ground forces might be an attractive bargain, which all parties could proclaim to be "balanced." But this presumably is for some later stage of the talks, if ever.

The asymmetry between the United States and the Soviet Union in terms of distance from the Central European front is commonly cited as a major unbalancing element in force reductions. Soviet forces withdrawing a few hundred miles by land can more readily be redeployed than can U.S. troops that have moved back three thousand miles, even if allowance is made for a transatlantic airlift capability. Thus unequal reductions, or a weighting of numbers by distance, may be necessary to attain true equivalence. Even then, it is sometimes argued, the Soviets could shift their recalled forces to the northern or southern NATO flank within the territory of the USSR, thereby creating new imbalances in Europe.

But although these approaches may be debatable, they lead logically to the conclusion that force reductions are either too complicated to be negotiated or too risky to be undertaken. But since NATO and the Soviets have agreed that the effort will be made, since the continuing presence of U.S. troops in Europe has been linked to the talks, and since Western public opinion is not likely to countenance the talks' abandonment before the possibilities have been explored, the matter cannot be wished away. And there is room for skepticism about both the complexities and the dangers of mutual force reductions.

For one thing, if the USSR now expects to gain security advantages from mutual force reductions, that vision did not come quickly to Moscow. The original NATO proposal was made in 1968. It was not picked up by the Warsaw Pact countries until 1970 and was not given explicit support until General Secretary Leonid Brezhnev's speech at Tiflis in May 1971. What impelled the Soviet leadership eventually to decide in favor of a negotiation can only be a matter for speculation. One possibility is that the Soviets have domestic reasons for wanting to demobilize a part of their Eastern European garrisons. Their thirty-one divisions (in East Germany, Poland, Hungary, and Czechoslovakia) may be excessive for police duty, which is their major task. The Soviet economy has a chronic problem of overly full employment, and it is always in need of civilian manpower, particularly manpower that has had experience with mechanical equipment. Even a modest contribution from the military forces in Central Europe probably would be welcome to the economic planners in Moscow. Balance-of-payments problems associated with the forces in Eastern Europe could be a further reason for considering a partial withdrawal. Another might be a hope that the discussions would give the Soviets a position from which to try to divide the members of NATO. On the other hand, some groups in Moscow may want to be able to reinforce Soviet troops on the Chinese border and may consider mutual force reductions in

Central Europe a safe and economical way of achieving this capability. Moscow may well prefer mutual force reductions to the unsettled situation in Europe that could follow from unilateral U.S. troop reductions in the central region. Or it may just be that the Soviets have no preconceptions at all but consider their participation as one element in a bargain, the other of which was the West's acceptance of a CSCE.

Any of these points might account for the apparent Soviet change of attitude. What is hardly plausible is the idea that the Soviet leaders could be entering into the negotiations having in mind an elaborate charade of troop reductions on one front in order to threaten NATO on another or surreptitiously to reintroduce forces on the central front after Western troop strength there had been cut. A military motive for such a bald act of bad faith is obscure enough, but the political reasoning that would have to lie behind it is even more so, for this action could reverse the whole trend toward détente and could restore the cold war with all its chill.

Surely the key point is that if and when force reductions do occur, a new political climate will have been created in Central Europe. Redeployment of Soviet troops thereafter, in any way threatening to NATO countries, would be bound to increase tensions, possibly to a very high degree. If the Soviets have in mind restoring a cold war atmosphere, or worse, it would be pointless to try to accomplish this through a policy of public duplicity.

It is quite possible, to be sure, that the USSR would in due course decide to restore troop strength in the regions where reductions had been made, for no agreement could be counted on to freeze everything forever. A redeployment could hardly take place in secret, however, although it probably could be managed more promptly and easily than could the reintroduction of U.S. forces. Its purpose might be to deal with unrest in Eastern Europe or to pressure the West. In either case it would be a deliberate choice, taking into account the military and political risks and costs, just as would be a decision, *which could after all be taken now,* to augment substantially the Soviet forces adjacent to the NATO region. But the difference would be that the NATO allies would receive notice somewhat earlier than would be true at present, the gravity of the Soviet decision would be more apparent, and a united allied response would therefore be easier to achieve.

A further consideration is that the pace of negotiated force reduction is within Western control. Discussions thus far strongly suggest that there is no risk of overly hasty agreement on either side. Both agree on the need for "the most effective and thorough approach to the consideration of the subject matter" and on the view that the "specific arrangements will have to be carefully worked out in scope and timing in such a way that they will *in all respects* and *at every point* conform to the principle of undiminished security for each party."[7] These are not the words or decisions of rash and imprudent negotiators.

This approach suggests that concerns about the complexity of the problem can be overdrawn as well. There is no way to measure mathematically abstractions like "balance" or "undiminished security." But small initial reductions in numbers of men and equipment, with accompanying safeguards and assurances (notification of maneuvers, exchange of observers, verification procedures), could get the process under way. Thereafter, on the key assumption that the Soviet Union is serious about reducing the scope and level of the military confrontation in Central Europe, the negotiation might acquire its own dynamic force; like SALT, it could go on in phases over a number of years, perhaps beyond the 1970s; it might proceed from modest force reductions to more complex systems of arms control and safeguards and to a multilateral consideration of the nuclear weapons in Europe. Like SALT also, the military steps could be associated with the pace of political change in Eastern Europe and the growth of confidence in the durability of European détente. Only when force reductions are thought of in terms of sudden and major changes out of political context does the problem of measuring a new balance become intolerably difficult.

Nevertheless, even mildly optimistic expectations for the force reduction negotiations would be premature. Both the NATO states and the Soviet Union are cautious about changing the status quo. The technical problems are substantial, and in the absence of strong political pressures for agreement, they will lead to long-drawn-out discussion and delay. It may well be that the time for mutual force reductions has not come and that the talks will eventually fail for lack of political will to make them succeed, or will achieve only small and marginal results.

Alternatively, the talks may fail because of the sheer complexity of the negotiating process, even though there is some will to achieve mutual reductions on both sides. In this case, the way out may be to move toward tacit agreement—by mutual example. The United States might probe this possibility, if formal agreement cannot be reached after several years of negotiation, by announcing a small unilateral withdrawal—and by indicating that further movement will hinge on Soviet reciprocity. The initial U.S. withdrawal might be geared to the moderately reduced needs of the short-war concept

7. Preparatory consultations for negotiations on mutual reduction of forces and armaments, final communiqué, June 28, 1973, point 3. (Emphasis added.)

outlined earlier. A negotiated agreement would be greatly preferable, however, since it could include the collateral restraints discussed above.

It will be essential in all this to maintain agreement among the allies. Proposals should be put to the Soviets—whether for explicit agreement or implicit
interaction—only if that agreement is forthcoming. Otherwise, the mere fact
that the proposals were made would do more damage to allied defense and
cooperation in nonmilitary fields than could be offset by any foreseeable
mutual withdrawals. For these withdrawals are likely to be limited by the fact
that the forces of both sides serve important political purposes. The Soviets
will need to maintain their forces to secure their control in Eastern Europe;
U.S. forces are needed to balance the large German forces (whose dominance
in any Western European military effort could create concerns that would do
much to unhinge Western European concert), and to provide tangible assurance of U.S. commitment. These facts make it likely that mutual withdrawals,
however helpful in a symbolic sense, will still leave large numbers of forces on
both sides. Indeed, the so-called collateral measures—safeguards against surprise attack and the like—may well in the end do more than troop withdrawals
to stabilize the situation in Europe by raising new barriers to the use of force,
thus reducing fear of that use.

These considerations will make it easier to maintain allied unity concerning
negotiations about mutual withdrawals. So long as these withdrawals seem
likely to take place within well-defined limits and in conjunction with collateral assurances, the Western European countries need not feel that their
survival is endangered. If a critical challenge to U.S.-European concert is
posed, it seems more likely to emerge on other fronts—notably that of economic policy. To this we now turn.

CHAPTER SEVEN

TRADE AND MONEY

Probably no proposition about the Atlantic relationship has been more assiduously promoted in popular commentaries and less well founded in substance than the view that there are fundamental conflicts of economic interest between Western Europe and North America. A whole lexicon of terms drawn from the vocabulary of war is commonly applied to international economic relations. Thus we hear about trade "offensives," economic "invasions," and monetary "battles." Persistence of this kind of terminology, and the underlying conception it represents, flies in the face of some obvious considerations: if actual losses were being inflicted on the participants, world trade would quickly dry up; investment flows would stop if there were no benefits to investors and recipients alike; international monetary arrangements that did not suit the interests of the nations involved would not last very long. Nonetheless, governments often act or threaten to act as if economic relations were indeed a species of belligerency. And there can be no doubt that economic differences and disputes, whatever their intrinsic merits, do in the end affect international political affairs and can endanger the whole structure of international relations.

A principal reason for this apparent paradox is, of course, that national politics consist of particular and local, as well as general, interests. Thus the European Community's agricultural policy has survived not because it brought cheap and abundant food to the consumer or because it led to an efficient use of Western European agricultural resources, but because it promised to deal with the genuine social and economic problems of the farm sector and because nothing unequivocally better has been offered. The American textile industry, to mention another important case, has been able to get government support against import competition on essentially similar grounds. Again, much of the apparently widespread hostility toward foreign direct investment can be attributed to the difficulties encountered by domestic business that has found itself exposed to additional competition, and from outsiders at that. Democratic governments are understandably responsive to pressures from these individual economic sectors, particularly if they contain large numbers of voters, whereas the larger social or community interest typically has fewer articulate and persuasive proponents. So it is not surprising that economic relations can generate issues involving heated attitudes and extravagant language, for very real, if rarely national, interests are often at stake.

The considerable successes that have nonetheless been achieved in building and strengthening the postwar international economic order have been made possible in no small part because potential benefits to some local interests have neutralized or offset the opposition of others. The marked reduction of trade barriers that has taken place since the end of World War II could only have happened in a circumstance in which one set of particular interests could be played off against another. Tariffs could be reduced in country A because its exporters knew that otherwise country B would not open its market. Direct investment similarly has continued to flow, in spite of much-publicized opposition in the receiving countries, because it has appeared to bring in its train additional employment, technical advances, or other advantages compelling to some groups or sectors. The international monetary system in force prior to 1971 seemed to many non-Americans unfairly skewed in favor of the United States but it was also associated with economic growth and prosperity and this served greatly to blunt the impact of its critics.

There is every reason to expect that further steps toward a more efficient and responsive system of economic relations in the world will depend essentially on the process of trading or appearing to trade particular benefits. The proper task of politicians and officials in this situation, arguably, is to discern and promote the tradeoffs and the bargains that will foster stability and prosperity on as wide a scale as may be possible at the time. It would be useless to believe that politicians anywhere will be able to ignore the views of major domestic interest groups. But experience suggests that progress is not thereby foreclosed. There is no compelling reason to suppose that most of the outstanding economic issues in the Atlantic region are not susceptible of compromise and resolution, as in the past. In fact, serious negotiations on economic questions have gone on throughout the past few years, even when much of the postwar international economic structure seemed to be in danger of collapse. It is overwhelmingly probable that discussion and negotiation will continue and that, at the least, outrightly foolish and self-defeating choices and actions mostly will be avoided. How far beyond that the Atlantic nations can go, with Japan and others, toward improved management of economic interdependence remains to be seen. Certainly, however, the cause is far from hopeless.

In this chapter, two key questions—money and trade—are examined in the light of the foregoing comments. Chapter 8 will then treat three others: investment, energy, and North-South relations.

International Monetary Reform

If proof is needed that the world's industrial economies are linked inextricably together, it is to be found in the record of international monetary arrangements since World War II.

From the end of the war until August 1971, the charter written at Bretton Woods in 1944 provided the basis for the international monetary system. The central feature of the Bretton Woods agreement was its emphasis on fixed exchange rates which would be adjustable only when a currency's declared par value had come to be "fundamentally" out of line with other currencies. This emphasis reflected the unhappy memories of the 1930s as well as the belief that traders and investors needed the assurance that would be provided by stable currency values. As the system developed, it became a cardinal point that the American dollar's parity was not to be altered by U.S. action, virtually no matter what; a devaluation of the dollar to correct a chronic deficit in the United States balance of payments thus was generally assumed to be out of the question.

There were good reasons for the Bretton Woods system and for the way in which it evolved. The monetary experience of the 1930s had been disastrous. International trade and investment is facilitated by stable currencies, everything else being equal. Since the American dollar represented claims on the world's preeminently productive economy, it was quite naturally adopted as the key currency, to be used as a reserve and as the chief monetary means for conducting international business. And the implicit assurance that the United States would not arbitrarily change the dollar's exchange value was a logical consequence of its use as a monetary reserve.

Anyway, as measured by results, the Bretton Woods system was a remarkable success. The postwar period was one of unprecedented growth in real output and in international exchanges of goods, services, and capital. The two developments were interrelated, and they were sustained and assisted by the large degree of order and freedom in the international economy, to which Bretton Woods undoubtedly made a crucial contribution.

The eventual breakdown of the system was nevertheless probably inevitable. Structural changes in the principal economies made some currencies too cheap and others too dear in their international transactions. The commitment to try to sustain officially declared currency values gave a license to speculators to make easy gains serving little social purpose. And as the industrial countries lurched from one currency crisis to another, the strains on intergovernmental relations heightened. Even though the major countries returned again and again to patchwork repairs of the monetary regime, simply because of the belief that otherwise prosperity would be threatened, these strains finally became too great. In 1971, the U.S. government did the unthinkable by overtly abandoning a fixed value for the dollar.

It is instructive to note that this, the single most shattering economic decision of the era, was followed promptly by agreement that a new system had to be created to replace the old one. No government, however vocal its unhappiness over the unilateral U.S. action, was prepared to say that it could do without *any* understandings on international monetary affairs. And in fact the initial discussions in the International Monetary Fund (IMF) uncovered a substantial area of agreement on basic principles.

In effect, the case was widely accepted for more flexible exchange rates among the major currencies, or groups of currencies. It was assumed that an effective coordination of national monetary policies could not soon be achieved; that in its absence, flexible exchange rates could in some degree insulate individual domestic economic policies from each other. Any return to fixed rates in all industrial countries on the Bretton Woods model was deemed to be out of the question for a long time to come. Henceforth, changes in currency values would be a usual, rather than a last-ditch, method of correcting balance-of-payments deficits and surpluses.

Even as the principle of flexibility was becoming accepted, continuing uncertainties in exchange markets led to an unplanned experiment with unpegged—floating—exchange rates among the major currencies, including a group of European currencies floating in common against all other currencies. And this experiment had been under way for less than a year when the explosion of petroleum prices confronted the industrial countries with a balance-of-payments situation of an unprecedented kind. It quickly became clear that very large trade deficits would be the rule and that novel problems of financing current imports would have to be dealt with. Monetary reform as a matter of formal negotiation was tacitly shelved, while governments turned to the short-term financial implications of the extraordinary increases in the costs of oil.

An obvious point was that flexible or floating exchange rates would not be sufficient to deal with the new circumstances. To allow exchange rates to fall as trade deficits mounted would raise further the domestic price of imported oil, something no government could contemplate cheerfully. Moreover, a significant devaluation in one country might set off a round of competitive devaluations that would hurt everyone. So some other means of coping with deficits would be needed. Countries with large exchange reserves could draw them down, but most would have to begin foreign borrowing promptly. This meant, in essence, obtaining access to the return flows of funds from the oil-producing countries. Since these funds were likely to go mainly to such established capital markets as London and New York, the "recycling" problem was one of assuring that deficit countries generally could get financing on tolerable terms. Initially, dependence could be placed on private lending facilities. But the sums were so large in relation to the risk-taking capacities of the private banks that it was implicitly understood from the first that intergovernmental cooperation would be required to avoid the danger of a breakdown—and in due course this was undertaken, once more in recognition of the inherent interdependence of the chief economies.

It is all but certain that there will be a return to the search for an agreed monetary system, as the oil financing problem subsides. Again, the issues to be resolved will be *how* to organize and manage a cooperative effort, not *whether* to cooperate.

One broad area of choice will be to continue with a flexible/floating system. Its appeal will be to allow governments greater freedom to decide on their domestic monetary and fiscal policies in the face of balance-of-payments difficulties and it seems likely to be adopted for that reason. But since nobody would suppose that governments would stand wholly aloof from so sensitive a question as exchange rates, there will still be needed close understandings and doubtless multilateral surveillance of any regime based on flexible or floating currency values. That is to say, the international community will have to have a voice in national decisions on exchange rates in any system that might actually be put into place.

The chief alternative to a flexible system will be an undertaking to go back to relatively stable exchange rates on the basis of commitments to coordinate closely domestic economic policies. It is possible that the inflationary experience of the first half of the 1970s will make attractive the idea of restoring the so-called balance-of-payments discipline over internal policy choices. If so, the need will be to find ways to assure that coordination of domestic policies is achieved, not merely talked about, else the structure will quickly break down. Taken literally, however, this is an extremely far-reaching idea and its prospects must be considered to be small as against a flexible system with an underpinning of international guidelines and institutional arrangements.

In either case—or if a compromise emerges between flexibility and domestic policy coordination—the outcome will be to advance the trend toward international intervention in national decisionmaking. Governments will accept this, even though it will impinge on national policies directly related to so sensitive a political matter as employment, because the alternative of having no international system simply will be unacceptable to even the most sovereignty-conscious of politicians.

Agricultural Trade and Industrial Tariffs

In spite of all that has happened since the end of the Kennedy Round, the trade issues directly between the United States and Western Europe are relatively unchanged. They are the conditions of agricultural trade, tariffs and tariff discrimination, and nontariff distortions of trade, all of which are related to access to markets. What has been added is the question of access to supplies.

Agriculture

For some time now, world agricultural markets have been dominated by shortages. The older problems of market access for efficient producers have been secondary. This is almost certainly temporary. Agricultural productivity has not stopped increasing, nor is effective demand likely to expand at a rate that will continue to put inordinate pressure on the supplies of most farm products.[1] At some time in the near future, the old problem of surpluses may reappear, and with them export subsidies, competitive dumping, and abrasive international relations.

One new factor is to be reckoned with, however. The ill-advised U.S. action in imposing official controls on exports of soybeans in the summer of 1973 and the generally tight markets for agricultural commodities of 1972-74 have left a legacy of apprehension about the future security of supply of agricultural imports. Whereas a few years ago the U.S.-European agricultural trade

1. This is said without prejudice to the serious and chronic food problems of many of the developing countries. While it is true that food requirements in the less developed countries (LDCs) as a whole cannot now be met adequately by indigenous farm production, it is also true that adequate diets are not likely to be achieved on a permanent basis by dependence on outside resources, even if it were possible to provide food on a gift rather than a commercial basis. The amounts are too large. A long-term answer must be found in a more productive indigenous LDC agriculture.

problem could be looked at solely as one of improving market access for efficient suppliers, it now has a further dimension, that of assuring consumers that exports will be available.

In this, there are the elements of a bargain. On the one hand, the United States, Canada, and Australia have an important interest in improving the future conditions of access to the European Community market for cereals and other products. On the other, the Community as an importer can reasonably ask for assurances that in all predictable situations its normal requirements will be met.

Access to the Community market, in the last analysis, depends on support prices in Europe. If these prices are above world prices, the Community will be impelled to protect them by its import levies. The key is to find a basis for gradually reducing supports within politically acceptable limits. During the Kennedy Round the Community offered the *montant de soutien*—level of support concept—as a basis for discussion. In effect, the idea was to determine actual levels of domestic support in comparison with some agreed world base price and to bargain about narrowing the difference. Although it was not pursued in the Kennedy Round, the *montant de soutien* approach is worth reviving. Under it, the participants in a negotiation might first agree to freeze margins of protection (that is, the difference between the domestic support level and the world price) and thereafter gradually to reduce them—that is, to allow support prices to decline slowly in real terms.

In the Community, where consumer preference gradually must pull the farm economy toward the production of animal protein, particularly beef, a downward movement in real prices for cereals, including feed grains, would strengthen these basic market forces. A slow and by no means enormous shift out of grain and into animal protein production would thus be consistent with consumer welfare. It also would be consistent with the Community's entirely legitimate objective of maintaining healthy agricultural sectors among the nine member countries. Furthermore, a negotiation on margins of protection and market access would have to include the heavily protected farm sectors in the United States, Canada, and elsewhere. A notable case is the North American dairy industry, which would have to be subjected to tests no different in principle than those applied to cereal production in Western Europe.

As for security of supply, the ultimate requirement is that physical stocks be available for use when supplies become scarce. Once a sufficiently bad harvest has hit the world, only stocks in being can make up the resulting shortfall. The prospect for successful negotiations to establish an international food reserve look brighter in the wake of the 1974 World Food Conference at Rome.

Heretofore the United States and Canada, alone among cereal producers, have held large stocks, and they have done so in order to sustain domestic prices against the pressure of surplus supplies. It is possible that the North American countries will again find themselves building and holding stocks because domestic considerations will make them do so. But this is not only not certain, it is unlikely. If there were to be a serious negotiation about market access, however, there would seem to be no overriding reason why it should not be related to the parallel international program for deliberate stockbuilding—mainly of cereal grains but possibly also of oilseeds and some other commodities, on a shared basis. Indeed, it is not easy to see how a negotiation about access can succeed without a security of supply feature. As a result of the international food reserve negotiation, each participant might agree to acquire and hold stocks, with target amounts fixed according to some agreed formula based on output or consumption data. There could be predetermined guidelines for releases of stocks, or a price trigger could be set. Buffer stock operations to iron out year-to-year fluctuations in price could be a part of the general agreement; that is, members would contract to add to stocks in times when output was above the trend and to sell when crops fell below average.

If progress is made in negotiations regarding an international food reserve, prospects for a market access-security of supply agreement will be enhanced. This could be an international bargain between the Community, the United States, Canada, Australia, and Japan; but others, notably the USSR, might be compelled by their interest in stable supplies to undertake the commitments and obligations involved. If agreement could be achieved, it would call for continuing and close collaboration covering exchanges of information on crops, consultation on market conditions, and joint decisionmaking.

The foregoing suggests that whereas agricultural trade has been a force pushing North America and Western Europe apart, it could now become a factor drawing the two sides of the Atlantic together. An agreement of the kind outlined here would be far from easy to accomplish. Still, at a time when a world food shortage and high prices have reduced the old strains and tensions over agricultural trade, it should be feasible to examine the possibilities for better use of agricultural resources in a more favorable political and economic climate. And by now, it may be hoped, a better understanding of political necessities may have led to a better grasp of what is politically practicable, which is the first necessary step toward a successful bargain.

Industrial Tariffs

Contrary to some opinion, tariffs on industrial products have not been reduced to inconsequential levels. Average duties in the major industrial countries range from 6 percent to 12 percent, with many sectoral and individual rates at much higher levels, and there are wide disparities in the tariff treatment of the same products in different countries. Trade and investment flows in the industrial world are still arbitrarily affected and distorted by tariffs. The less developed countries are seriously handicapped by the tariffs of rich nations, which tend to bear most heavily on labor-intensive manufactures. And tariff issues create disputes among industrial countries, with effects that can spill over into the areas of political and defense policy. In short, the case for a new round of tariff cuts is a very strong one.

Beyond these broad considerations, there is the issue of tariff discrimination. As a customs union, the European Community is inherently discriminatory in that internal tariffs have been removed and a common tariff is applied to imports from nonmembers. Customs unions are permitted under the General Agreement on Tariffs and Trade (GATT), of course, and the Community's customs union is further justified as a step toward the larger political goal of European unification. Even so, the Kennedy Round was in large part a necessary means of making more acceptable to the rest of the world the discriminatory trade impact of the common external tariff of the Six.[2] But with the enlargement and the extension of the European Community's preferential system, the problem of discrimination remains very much alive.

The Community's controversial preferential trade arrangements with nonmember countries have differing justifications. One group of agreements is with developing countries, initially the African dependencies or former colonies of the member states. These agreements, which were originally embodied in the so-called Yaoundé Convention,[3] were intended to prevent a damaging rupture of the special trade ties between the former dependencies and the metropoles. As a result of the Community's accession agreement with the United Kingdom, the Yaoundé system has been extended in the Lomé Convention which links forty-six developing nations in Africa, the Caribbean, and the Pacific with the Community in special trade and aid agreements. These include a novel plan for the stabilization of earnings from primary commodity

---

2. A customs union, of course, may also be trade-creating through its effects on economic growth and income. See Lawrence B. Krause, *European Economic Integration and the United States* (Brookings Institution, 1968).

3. The original agreement was entered into in 1958 and was extended in 1964 and again in 1969 at Yaoundé in Cameroon.

exports.[4] An important modification in the new convention is the dropping of the controversial "reverse" tariff preferences granted by the associated states to the Community.

In the Mediterranean area a series of preferential trade arrangements are sometimes cited as the beginnings of a Community "Mediterranean policy."[5] Association agreements with Greece and Turkey were entered into in 1962 and 1963. In these cases, the envisaged goal was full Community membership after rather long transitional periods. Morocco and Tunisia (which had earlier preferential relations with France), as well as Spain, Israel, and Malta, have since signed special trade treaties with the EC. These are justified on the basis of "traditional" economic ties and also on political grounds—the so-called Mediterranean policy.

The more important preferential agreements are those covering Sweden, Switzerland, Finland, Austria, Portugal, Iceland, and Norway. These agreements provide for the achievement by stages of industrial free trade, with some exceptions, by 1977—or by 1980 for Portugal and Iceland. If carried out, they would lead to a Western European free trade area. For these members of the European Free Trade Association (EFTA), which had $47 billion of trade (in 1972) with the members of the enlarged Community and which faced the loss of their free access to the U.K. market, the Community trade agreements are of great importance. On the Community's side, the nine members had varying but impelling commercial and political reasons for wanting to minimize barriers to trade with these neighbors and trading partners.

Thus, as seen through Community eyes, the trading arrangements are tailored to specific and demanding requirements: to give continuing market access to the economically weak dependencies and former colonies; to construct a common Western European policy toward the important Mediterranean region; and to minimize trade disruptions within Western Europe as enlargement proceeds.

Looked at from outside the Community, the preferential arrangements represent a major breach in the postwar trading system. Article 1 of the

4. European Community Information Service, "ACP Treaty Ready for Signature," press release, no. 6 (Washington, D.C., February 13, 1975; revised).

5. As former EC Commission President Franco Malfatti said, "It is clear that such agreements are a first step towards an increased European presence in the Mediterranean area, as a factor for equilibrium and peace. I do not believe that anyone can contest the constructive role that can be played in Europe in relieving the strains and pressures felt by the countries bordering the Mediterranean." European Community Information Service, "The European Community and the United States, 1972," Background Information, no. 15 (Washington, D.C., June 1972).

GATT, which makes nondiscrimination the rule for trade among the countries adhering to the agreement, seems to have been set aside on a wholesale basis. Although the volume of nonmember trade at stake in Africa and the Mediterranean is relatively small, the apparent violation of a fundamental GATT principle has caused more concern, particularly in the United States, than the European Community has generally recognized. As former U.S. Secretary of Agriculture Hardin told a presidential commission in 1970, "The grave danger is that as a result of the present plans for enlarging the Community, European and African nations will have created a trading area sufficiently large to enable them to depart entirely from MFN [most-favored-nation] treatment and will plunge the rest of the world into a trade jungle in which special deals become the practice rather than the exception, and in which spheres of trading influence will develop as a matter of course."[6] Now that the Community has its special trade arrangements with the Western European neutral countries plus Portugal and Iceland, which together accounted for more than 13 percent of American exports to Western Europe in 1972, the concern, if anything, has increased.

This situation contains the danger of a classic confrontation. The Community has entered into political and legal commitments of a binding nature, which Brussels cannot undo unilaterally. From the point of view of the United States and others, these commitments contravene a key international rule and threaten important commercial interests. Both sides can present strong arguments, based on principle and on practice, to support their stands. If the issue cannot be resolved, there could be a trend toward fragmentation—with the United States and Japan staking out preferential positions in Latin America and Southeast Asia, respectively, to offset the European-African-Mediterranean bloc. This fragmentation not only would create growing disputes among the developed countries; it would also retard growth in the developing nations by denying them access to worldwide trade.

These opposing positions cannot be reconciled by an appeal to GATT legalities. GATT procedures, which call for the multilateral consideration of complaints, are not well suited to settlement of disputes between the major trading powers. And GATT remedies—retaliatory trade measures—would only make differences more irreconcilable. The only way out would be to reduce or eliminate the reasons for the disputes. If tariffs among the industrial coun-

6. Clifford M. Hardin, "Needed—A Market-Oriented Agricultural Trading World," in *United States International Economic Policy in an Interdependent World,* vol. I, Papers submitted to the Commission on International Trade and Investment Policy (U.S. Government Printing Office, 1971), pp. 799-800.

tries can be lowered and eventually abolished, the problem of discrimination will diminish and then disappear entirely, along with the tariffs themselves.

Gradual progress toward zero tariffs among the principal industrial countries is not a particularly new or radical idea. It was provided for in the U.S. trade legislation of 1962, and authority to negotiate to this end was included in former President Nixon's proposed Trade Reform Act of 1973. The experiences of both the Community and the European Free Trade Association, whose members had differing industrial structures and initial tariff levels, showed that tariffs could be removed, and in advance of the original ten-year schedule at that, without serious difficulty. Although the elimination of tariffs evidently cannot be made a goal of the forthcoming GATT round—because of both the reluctance of the Community and the unwillingness of the U.S. Congress to grant the necessary authority—it should be an objective of a later effort, perhaps toward the end of the seventies, and should be even now a long-term objective.

In any event, industrial tariffs will be a central issue in the upcoming trade negotiation, with the United States, the European Community, and Japan as the principal protagonists. There are complicated questions as to how to proceed—whether to cut all tariffs equally, to "harmonize" tariffs at lower levels, or to negotiate sectoral tariff agreements. These will have to be resolved by a compromise that includes something of each. This need not delay the negotiation; but often procedural questions become political sticking points and frustrate an enterprise that is badly needed to supplant the bickering over particular trade issues that has characterized the recent past.

Nontariff Distortions

Among the subjects of the current international debate, the so-called nontariff barriers (more accurately, nontariff distortions of trade) usually have been treated in a simplistic and hortatory way, which has tended to confuse rather than to enlighten. In reality, the nontariff measures are complicated, undramatic, and, despite the recent attention given to them, for the most part not new. Nor are they exclusive to any one country or group of countries. When the GATT secretariat undertook in 1967 to assemble a list of existing nontariff barriers, the result was a compilation of more than eight hundred items, quite evenly distributed among all the contracting parties.[7]

What we refer to as nontariff barriers are such familiar measures as import quotas; restrictions on government purchases; export subsidies; burdensome

7. Gardner Patterson, "Current GATT Work on Trade Barriers," in ibid., p. 621.

customs procedures and rules; industrial safety, health, and environmental standards; technically complex arrangements like border adjustments for sales and excise taxes; and, most recently, controls on exports in short supply. All nations apply some or all of these measures in ways that interfere with or distort international commerce. And their range may indeed be broadening.[8] Within the European Community and in EFTA, discussions have been held about removing some of these barriers on a regional basis,[9] which could raise new issues of trade discrimination.

Any multilateral effort to check the unraveling of world trade relationships will need to deal with nontariff distortions. They are burdensome in themselves, and if some are to be reduced or eliminated only within Western Europe, quarrels over them will be worsened. Most of the distortions, however, are imbedded in law or regulation or have their roots in long-standing national policies. For the United States, with its nontariff measures usually based on statutes, congressional action will be necessary before international bargains can be completed. (A Kennedy Round agreement in this field foundered when the U.S. Congress refused to repeal the law calling for special valuation procedures—the so-called American Selling Price—on certain chemicals.) In the new U.S. trade bill enacted last year the President was given authority to negotiate on nontariff measures, subject to congressional veto power.

Scattered through the GATT are provisions dealing with nontariff trade measures. Article 3 treats internal taxes, Article 7 covers customs valuation, Article 11 outlaws quantitative restrictions, Article 16 prescribes limits on export subsidies, and so on. The whole purpose of the GATT, of course, is to put mutually agreed-upon restraints on arbitrary or discriminatory governmental measures, tariff or nontariff, that distort the conditions of international trade. The existing provisions of the GATT, with interpretive notes or protocols to make them more precise, plus new protocols on public procurement and standards, would largely cover the nontariff field. There would still be need, however, for improved dispute-resolving machinery in the GATT. The present procedures, which in principle can engage the entire membership, are cumbersome and hopelessly slow. A permanent panel—or panels—of experts to recommend on disputes, to mediate, and to build up a body of precedent would be a necessary supplement to a renovation of the GATT's rules.

8. Robert E. Baldwin, *Nontariff Distortions of International Trade* (Brookings Institution, 1970), chap. 1.
9. Gerard and Victoria Curzon, *Global Assault on Non-Tariff Trade Barriers* (London: Trade Policy Research Centre, 1972), chap. 2.

In brief, the nontariff problem requires additional commitments to a system of rules and procedures governing international trade. Nothing revolutionary is involved, not even an effort to rewrite the GATT (an effort that could not succeed under voting procedures that give each of the eighty-odd contracting parties virtually an equal vote). Western Europe, the United States and Canada, and Japan could themselves produce a set of agreed interpretations to modernize the GATT charter. Whether other contracting parties would want to associate themselves with the work and to accept the new obligations could be left open. In the first instance, however, priority should be given to restoring and extending order and restraint among the major trading nations. Their example could not fail over time to be pervasive throughout the GATT membership.

Access to Supplies

Finally, there is the question of access to supplies. Cutbacks in exports by the oil-producing countries have made this seem to be the most urgent of trade problems. Concern is widespread, moreover, that other primary materials will also be withheld in the future, mainly by developing countries. And U.S. export controls on oilseeds in the summer of 1973 showed that even long existing trade channels within the developed world could be blocked when the perceived priority need was to curb domestic inflation.

Unfortunately it is probably true that GATT rules and commercial policy measures have potentially little bearing on the oil supply problem. The handful of countries that actually limit exports of oil are not likely to agree that international codes in any way restrict their freedom of action. Nor does the idea of concerted trade action against them by consuming nations hold out any real promise. Oil prices will eventually fall as demand for imports lags or declines and as alternative supplies come onto the market. Meanwhile, the buyers of oil can best improve their situation by joint measures to speed the work of market forces, discussed in the next chapter.

Whether concerns about other primary commodities are well founded is at least questionable. Most prices reached record or near-record levels in 1973 and early 1974 not because of artificial restrictions on supply but because demand had outrun the near-term possibilities for increasing output. As the balance between supply and demand changes, prices will stabilize. Some will fall. In that event, efforts by suppliers to bolster prices through a program of restrictions may well follow. But there are many obstacles in the path of those who try to construct primary product cartels. There is little reason to suppose that many could succeed.

Even so, an international community in which flows of traded goods—primary commodities or foodstuffs or manufactures—are liable to be arbitrarily shut off by supplying nations is patently not in very good shape. At present the international rules in this field are inadequate and should be strengthened. For foodstuffs it may be possible, as suggested above, to develop a system of reserve stocks to carry the world over periods of shortage. For other goods, the first requirement is that the industrial nations, which account for the bulk of world trade, put their own house in order by agreeing on a strict code to govern export controls. At a minimum, an exporting country with a short supply situation should be required to consult with the principal importers before applying export restrictions. This requirement alone would be an important step toward assuring fair sharing; but it would be well to go further and write into new rules a broad formula for sharing, with possible sanctions for failure to comply. It is unlikely that the developing countries would accept such a constraint initially, but the example might be salutary, and more adherents might be found in the course of time.

CHAPTER EIGHT

ENERGY, INVESTMENT, AND THE THIRD WORLD

Monetary and trade issues are long-standing items on the international agenda. The other major international economic questions do not fit so clearly into accustomed patterns. However, they share with money and trade the common characteristic of requiring, for their proper management, close and continuing multilateral cooperation. Also they have a large potential for political disruptiveness.

Imports of energy supplies are indispensable in almost all of the industrial states if present levels of economic activity are to be maintained. Foreign direct investment through multinational corporations has become an emotion-laden subject among the industrial nations, as well as in many of the less developed countries. Relations between the rich and the poor countries will have pervasive effects on the international scene for as long as can be foreseen; and the existing arrangements for cooperation among the rich countries and between the rich and the poor are far from satisfactory.

Energy Resources

The most critical recent development in Atlantic economic relationships has been in the area of energy supplies. Until quite recently the Western Hemisphere could serve as an ultimate source of supply when an oil shortage threatened Western Europe and Japan. As late as 1967, it was possible to increase U.S. output and to reduce U.S. imports by a total of some one hundred million barrels during the six months after the second closing of the Suez Canal.[1] Even before the current crisis, however, there was no excess capacity in the United States, the Western Hemisphere reserve was no more, the United States was rapidly expanding its imports of oil, and Western

1. Office of Business Economics, *1969 Business Statistics: 17th Biennial Edition,* A Supplement to the *Survey of Current Business* (1970), p. 167.

Europe's consumption had more than quintupled from 1957 levels. A projection of the trends at that time to 1980 would have shown imports of nine to ten million barrels a day into the United States, eighteen to twenty million barrels into Western Europe, and ten to eleven million barrels into Japan. And most of these supplies would have come from the Persian Gulf area, where the bulk of the world's oil reserves are located.

It was probable, therefore, that as the decade went on the oil-consuming areas all would be seeking increased petroleum supplies from a limited number of low-cost sources; a few countries—notably Iran and Saudi Arabia—would be the dominant suppliers. Since oil would be the principal source of energy and fuel supplies in every consuming country (including the developing countries, whose needs are rising also) well into the next decade, it was also evident that the producing countries might be able to exert upward pressures on price and that the conduct of normal economic activity everywhere would be uncomfortably dependent on continued imports.

The situation was further complicated by questions about the future role of the international oil companies, American and British, which produced, transported, refined, and marketed most of the oil for everyone. The fact that the United States was deeply engaged with the state of Israel generated reactions in the Arab countries that seemed to many to put the status of the oil companies in question; and there was the further problem of an obvious rise in the national aspirations of the producing countries to gain greater control over and returns from their oil resources. In Europe and Japan, therefore, there was concern over the ability of the companies to provide assured supplies of oil—a commodity that comes as close as any to being "vital." This was combined with preexisting misgivings about the place of these large foreign companies in the national economies of the consuming countries.

What had seemed an important evolving problem suddenly became an immediate crisis in October 1973. The Arab countries reduced their oil exports when the Arab-Israeli war broke out, and it seemed that the industrial world had entered a new era—that the long period of cheap and readily available energy raw materials had come to an abrupt end. In the early days of the use of the Arab "oil weapon," there was even concern that a real breakdown might occur in the economic life of the oil-dependent countries of Western Europe and Japan.

The worst fears aroused by the Arab action have not been realized, however. None of the major consuming countries, not even those temporarily subject to an embargo, have suffered anything close to a catastrophic reduction in oil supplies. They have faced inconvenience, rapid price increases, and certain industrial dislocations; but consumption levels seem to have adjusted to the higher oil prices. (In affluent societies the margin for cutting down on nonessential energy use is obviously large.) Industry, transport, and home heating have not been disrupted, and economic life has gone on without fundamental change. Nonetheless, the prospect is that oil prices that are high by past standards will continue for a lengthy period. More troubling still, it has been demonstrated that oil supplies from the Near East can be partially shut off at will. What had been feared over the years became a reality in 1973. The question of how to respond to this new situation is something that the Atlantic nations and Japan must face, either as a group or individually.

There are several aspects of the oil question. One, the problem of financing the current trade deficits attributable to high oil prices, was referred to in chapter 7. A second is the possibility of combined consumer action to bring oil prices down. The third is the need to plan against a new supply emergency.

In spite of everything, including a truly numbing volume of forecasts of disaster imminently at hand, the industrial nations' response to the upheaval in the oil market has been about as measured and sensible as might reasonably have been expected. The financing problem and the dangers in the sudden development of very large current-account deficits in the industrial world were recognized early; precautionary actions against critical national balance-of-payments situations were slower in coming, but then it was never probable that the Atlantic powers would fail to mount a rescue operation if one of them found itself unable to finance its essential imports. An "international energy program" which provides for common action, including sharing of supplies in the event of a general or selective oil embargo, was agreed upon by negotiators from sixteen countries in, by all usual standards, an astoundingly brief period. Cooperation to bring down prices is for the short run a matter of reduced oil consumption on the part of the big importing countries, and this has been agreed. Even though national austerity policies are almost bound to fall short of achieving cuts in imports that are sufficiently drastic to break oil cartel prices quickly, limited actions will support market forces that in any case are working strongly in the same direction.

Meanwhile, foolish and self-defeating ideas about policies on oil have received little support. Military intervention seems to have been excluded from the outset. Confrontation with the oil-producing states has been avoided. Attempts to find security in bilateral oil deals have been less extensive than might have been expected, if only because the costs have turned out to be very high for arrangements that would have given no guarantees of supplies anyway.

It would be overly optimistic to suppose that another oil emergency would not put new and perhaps severe strains on consumer country relations or even that the current period of high prices will wind down without further momentary "crises" in the Atlantic relationship. But events have not borne out the more apocalyptic visions of a breakdown of industrial country cooperation on account of a struggle for oil supplies. On the contrary, the dominant theme—represented to an unusual degree in the agreement to share scarce supplies—has been one of a commonality of interest among the industrial, oil-consuming nations.

This mirrors the underlying realities. The oil-consuming countries are linked together in fundamental ways. Any prolonged and serious shortage of energy supplies in Europe or Japan, whatever the cause, could be ignored by the United States only if existing military and security ties were considered to be meaningless. Such a shortage would soon have damaging effects on the economic and political life in all the oil-consuming countries. The United States is less vulnerable than the others now, and will probably remain so, but neither Western Europe nor Japan could be complacent about the economic and security consequences for themselves if there is a serious energy shortage in America. The industrial countries thus face a common need to assure that more oil sources will be found and developed, that substitute sources of energy will be created, that unavoidable shortfalls will be met by the reduction of nonessential use, and that emergency situations will evoke a planned series of responses. In these circumstances, the common interest of the consumer countries argues, if not for a single strategy, at least for agreement on a range of matters, including relations with the producing countries. It is not impossible that the oil-producing exporting countries' interest in remunerative prices eventually could be combined with the consumers' interest in assured supplies in a multilateral petroleum agreement. Common policies among the industrial countries could help to set the stage for such an agreement.

None of this is to say that the international energy problem is not a very serious one—merely to suggest that it is also a manageable one, and that concert among the Atlantic nations and Japan to this end is within our political reach.

Direct Investment and the Multinational Corporation

Oil is not the only area in which so-called multinational companies are in evidence. A powerful force for economic interdependence in the postwar years has been the flow of capital across national boundaries, particularly in the form of direct investment in plant and facilities by companies that operate in more than one country—that is, the multinational corporations. As a means of transferring capital, advanced technology, and managerial and scientific skills across national boundaries, and of integrating economic processes efficiently, the multinational firm is beyond doubt remarkably effective.[2] It is also a source of much uneasiness and tension in international relations, for it means that the locus of control of corporate activity is often at least nominally in another country. Although overt hostility toward the multinational corporation has been characteristic of developing countries, attitudes in the industrial countries have also become increasingly critical.

Foreign investment is a prime political issue in Canada and is perhaps the single most discussed aspect of U.S.-Canadian relations.[3] Until recently Japan allowed foreign direct investment only under restrictive, and from the investor's point of view, onerous conditions. In Western Europe there is a widespread and resentful view that U.S. multinational companies were able to "take over" European industry under a monetary system that allowed the United States to run balance-of-payments deficits without serious hindrance.[4]

The focus on American multinational corporations is understandable. U.S. private direct investment has increased very rapidly in the postwar years, with book value increasing roughly seven times, to $78 billion, between 1950 and 1970. In Western Europe and Canada, private direct investment was $5.3 billion in 1950 and $47.5 billion in 1970.[5] Even though Western European and

2. "Their [the multinational corporations] ability to tap financial, physical and human resources around the world and to combine them in economically feasible and commercially profitable activities, their capacity to develop new technology and skills and their productive and managerial ability to translate resources into specific outputs have proven to be outstanding." United Nations, Department of Economic and Social Affairs, *Multinational Corporations in World Development* (United Nations, 1973), p. 20.

3. Herbert Gray and others, *Foreign Direct Investment in Canada,* known as the Gray Report (Ottawa: Government of Canada, 1972), is a comprehensive examination of foreign investment issues from the point of view of a country that is host to a very large number of multinational companies.

4. General de Gaulle expressed this view in one of his carefully prepared press conferences: "It is true that there is an American foothold in some of our business enterprises. But we know that this is due in large part not so much to organic superiority of the United States as to the dollar inflation they export to others under cover of the gold-exchange standard.

"It is quite remarkable that the total of the American balance-of-payments deficit for the last eight years is precisely the same as the total for American investment in Western European countries." Reported in *New York Times,* November 28, 1967.

5. About $23 billion in Canada and more than $24 billion in Western Europe in 1970. U.S. Department of Commerce, *Policy Aspects of Foreign Investment by U.S. Multinational Corporations* (January 1972), p. 13.

Japanese multinational company investments have been growing in number and importance, the U.S. companies are still the dominant element.

Although there are large European and Japanese companies, there are more American giants.[6] The latter can devote sizable resources to research and development, and they are heavily represented in the advanced industries, especially in electronics, and in critical sectors like oil refining and distribution.[7] U.S. firms are said sometimes to ignore local employment practices. They may concentrate research activities (or export production) in their home country. Or they are subject to the policy control and direction of the government in Washington.[8] They are able to transfer funds from country to country to take advantage of impending changes in exchange rates. And finally, although it is official U.S. policy to welcome foreign investment, outsiders say that several obstacles limit their investment opportunities in the United States—for example, national or state restrictions that limit or prohibit foreign ownership control in a number of industries under antitrust legislation, and local taxes that are not covered by double taxation agreements.

Nor has skepticism about direct investment been confined to Canada or Europe or Japan. The American labor movement has been critical, sometimes bitterly so, of the multinational corporation as an "exporter" of domestic employment opportunities, and an undercurrent of hostility toward the multinationals is an evident fact of American political life.

How much weight is given to these kinds of concerns depends somewhat on the observer's point of view. In many countries where the multinational company in the abstract is looked on with suspicion, governments nevertheless still offer tax inducements to attract foreign investors, either to aid depressed regions, or as a general policy. As large as some multinational firms are, they are subject to the overriding tax and regulatory powers of national governments and are highly conscious that this is so. What is "speculation in foreign exchange markets" to an outsider is prudent management of a corporation's liquid balances to a multinational treasurer. The economic argument

6. See, for example, Jacques Servan-Schreiber, *The American Challenge* (Atheneum, 1958). See also Alastair Buchan, *The Implications of a European System for Defense Technology*, no. 6 of *Defence, Technology and the Western Alliance* (London: Institute for Strategic Studies, 1967), p. 7.

7. Christopher Layton, *Trans-Atlantic Investments* (Paris: Atlantic Institute, 1966), offers a balanced discussion of these points.

8. The United States has from time to time sought to apply its domestic policies (for example, controls on East-West trade, antitrust laws) unilaterally to American subsidiary companies in Canada and Western Europe. Whatever their intrinsic importance, these instances of extraterritoriality have justifiably aroused opposition and a suspicion that Washington policy control may extend to other, unpublicized areas.

for the multinational firm finds pragmatic support in the increasing volume of European and Japanese direct investments going to the United States.[9] These inflows, which cross outgoing American investments, obviously are in response to selective opportunities to provide skills, capital, and usually a differentiated product in foreign markets.

Also, of course, the industrial countries have an interest in equitable treatment for their direct investments in the developing countries—and thus a reason for mounting common efforts to try to meet the grievances of developing countries without abandoning direct investment as a way of promoting economic growth.

In the last analysis, few if any governments would prohibit foreign direct investment or change in any radical way the treatment of multinational corporations in their jurisdictions.[10] There is at least a presumptive case that direct investments help to raise incomes all around. Interfering with the process, therefore, would risk immediate economic losses as well as harm to external relations. Nevertheless, it makes sense for the industrial countries to conduct a systematic examination of direct investment issues in the Organisation for Economic Co-operation and Development (OECD). For the multinational corporation does raise important questions of public policy, notably about anticompetitive practices and about tax liabilities. Large firms, operating through subsidiaries in several countries, may well be able to frustrate official policies that are intended to enforce competition. Little would be gained if private trade barriers in the form of oligopolistic practices were to take the place of official trade restrictions, which have been greatly reduced in the postwar years. As for taxation, companies that are established in a number of jurisdictions may be able to pay their taxes in the country where the tax is lowest; or of course, they may be victims of double taxation.

Government policies concerning foreign investment also could stand greater international scrutiny. Investment incentives are an obscure area. Do they distort flows of trade and investment, at considerable social cost, or are they a valid means for accomplishing reasonable social goals? The extraterritorial application of national policies is a sore subject that cries out for sensible

9. Not too surprisingly, some U.S. reactions to foreign direct investment have ranged from "questioning" to "opposed," and the U.S. Senate has held hearings to determine the possible adverse effects of foreign ownership in the United States.

10. The United Nations says: "The key issue is not whether the home country should hamstring or do away with the multinational corporations, but how their behaviour may be influenced so as to correspond more closely to a set of enlightened national and international objectives." *Multinational Corporations in World Development*, p. 59.

accommodation. Investment relations with the developing countries present another whole set of problems. So does the question of common disclosure requirements for companies operating in the Atlantic world. It is possible that there can be no general program for dealing with the direct investment phenomenon, and that particular issues will have to be dealt with as they arise. It is also conceivable that a formal intergovernmental agreement would be needed to deal adequately with multinational firms. Only the kind of informational exchange that is possible in the OECD will give the Atlantic countries and Japan the basis for deciding how to preserve the undoubted advantages of foreign investment while ensuring against unacceptable intrusions on national sovereignties or abuses of economic power.

North-South Relations

As a practical matter, new economic directions for the world will be determined mainly by the core group of industrial countries, simply because of their productive capacities. An inescapable question is: how will the decisions and actions of these rich nations affect the much larger number of poor, less developed countries? A partial answer is that an economic order that promotes prosperity in the major trading countries will provide the best possible environment for material progress everywhere. But matters cannot be left there. Pressures for policies aimed more directly toward the LDCs are bound to intrude.

The rich nations of the world are publicly committed to aiding the economic and social development of the poor nations. When the OECD was created in 1960 to replace the earlier Organisation for European Economic Co-operation, economic development was put on a parity with stability and growth as a goal of the member nations.[11] Since then the commitment to help the less developed countries has been repeated regularly in official pronouncements[12] and in mutually agreed undertakings to provide aid and markets for the poor countries. The most striking is the UN target, adopted in 1968, of annual transfers by the economically advanced countries of 1 percent

11. *Convention on the Organisation for Economic Co-operation and Development* (Paris: OECD, 1960), Article 1.

12. The late President Georges Pompidou of France said on the occasion of the tenth anniversary of the OECD: "[The] privileged situation of the OECD countries involves duties, and duties of the utmost gravity. I am thinking here of their relations with the less developed countries. There is no more urgent need than that of supplying these countries with the aid which will enable them to cross the threshold after which progress becomes self-sustaining. This aid, if it is to be effective, must be substantial, it must be concentrated." *Atlantic Community*, vol. 9, no. 1 (Spring 1971), p. 122.

of their GNP to the less developed nations;[13] but other, less dramatic promises of more favorable trade conditions are also spread over the record.

The acceptance of collective responsibility by the developed nations for economic progress in the LDCs is one of the remarkable occurrences of the post-World War II years. Before the war, the idea of any common concern for world economic development, if it was entertained at all, had no status in national or international policies. The use of public money to assist other peoples' economic growth would have been unthinkable. Yet beginning with the charters of the United Nations and the International Bank for Reconstruction and Development (IBRD), development has come gradually to be recognized as a problem for the world community as well as for individual countries. Virtually all developed countries now have budgets and policies and official bodies devoted to it,[14] and a group of international institutions has been created to manage its collective aspects.

These developments no doubt reflect widely held humanitarian concepts, which are, however, mingled with considerations of a more material kind. President Robert S. McNamara of the World Bank Group has stated in quantitative terms the consequences of policies that neglect the poor countries: "At the end of the century—only a generation away—the people of the developed countries will be enjoying per capita incomes, in 1972 prices, of over $8,000 per year, while these masses of the poor (who by that time will total over 2¼ billion) will on the average receive less than $200 per capita and some 800 million of these will receive less than $100."[15] It is impossible to escape the conclusion that the kind of world thus forecast would be liable to aggravated political and social stresses. More particularly, the growing recognition that the preservation of a habitable planet will require food and environmental cooperation on a global basis injects a note of urgency into relations between the developed and the developing countries.

Unfortunately, awareness of the problem and statements of interest have not yet been matched by action. At this time it is highly probable that the official development aid target for the 1970s will be missed by a wide margin.[16]

13. The "target" was accepted in varying degrees; the United States and some others did not set target dates, and the U.S. "best efforts" pledge was to increase total flows of resources rather than to reach the 1 percent figure. See Organisation for Economic Co-operation and Development, Development Assistance Committee, *Development Assistance: Efforts and Policies* (Paris: OECD, 1971).

14. Goran Ohlin, *Foreign Aid Policies Reconsidered* (Paris: Development Centre of the Organisation for Economic Co-operation and Development, 1966), chap. 2.

15. International Bank for Reconstruction and Development, International Finance Corporation, International Development Association, *Summary Proceedings,* 1971 Annual Meeting of the Boards of Governors (Washington, D.C., September 25, 1972).

16. Ibid.

The foreign aid program of the largest donor—the United States—is dwindling, and increases elsewhere will not make up the difference. The United States, furthermore, is behind in its pledges to the international lending institutions, with no assurance that the necessary legislative action will be taken. In their trade policy toward the developing countries, the performance of the industrial countries can most charitably be described as lamentable.

The Need for Action

Renewed and innovative efforts clearly are desirable. This is especially so since the recent dramatic increases in the prices of oil, wheat, and other commodities threaten to have a critical impact on the prospects of the poorer developing nations, whose plight emphasizes the need for new short-term steps to meet the immediate crisis. Prominent among the latter are action to reduce the effective price paid by the poorest developing countries for wheat and oil—the two commodities whose price increases have dealt the developing countries the worst blow.

These price rises, of course, have different causes. Wheat prices have increased because bad crops in the USSR, South Asia, and North America have put heavy pressure on supplies. There is every reason to expect that the higher prices will lead to larger supplies. Oil prices have risen because supplies have been reduced by administrative decision. From the standpoint of the developing countries, however, the result is the same, and remedial action needs to be taken in both cases. This action might include interdependent decisions by the wheat- and oil-exporting countries to provide these commodities on concessional terms: payment by importing countries of the difference between pre-increase prices and current prices might be deferred for an extended time. It will also be necessary to take other near-term actions. For example, an effort might be made to direct the large sums being received by the oil-exporting countries to investment in the oil-importing developing nations. But the principal lesson of the current crisis is that it is more necessary than ever to press ahead toward dealing with the longer-term problems of the poor nations.

Critical among these is that of food production. Long-term projections suggest that world food production and effective demand will be in reasonable overall balance, but they also suggest a potentially disastrous regional imbalance: food production in the developed world will outrun demand; the reverse will be true in large parts of the developing world. Theoretically, this imbalance can be accommodated by international trade; in practice, its effects will be seriously adverse unless its extent can be mitigated by increased production in the developing nations. This requires large additional investment, as well as changes of policy by these nations. Some of the investment resources required will have to come from elsewhere—notably the industrial nations and the oil-exporting countries. At the 1974 World Food Conference it was proposed that an agricultural development fund be set up for this purpose. Translating this proposal into action and endowing the fund with substantial contributions from the Atlantic nations is a high priority need.

But even if the developing world's food production is greatly increased, it will not be self-sufficient. The developing nations will still have to pay for large food imports with other exports. And the bulk of those exports will have to be bought by the industrial nations. The forthcoming GATT trade negotiations offer a crucial opportunity to provide greater market access for the exports of developing countries. For more than a decade now, the international community has been interested in preferential trading systems—regional, as in the case of the agreements of the European Community as a whole, and generalized, as in the case of agreements among the industrial countries in which preferences are given to the developing countries as a group. Neither approach is calculated to satisfy the political and economic needs of the rich-poor relationship in the 1970s and beyond.

The logical result of regional trade preferences is a world divided into three North-South trading blocs: the United States and Canada with Latin America; Europe with Africa; and Japan with South and Southeast Asia. The dependency and neocolonial implications of such a world would not be happy ones for North-South political relationships; and the economic distortions would be particularly costly for the developing countries. Generalized tariff preferences that are sufficiently generous would avert these problems. But experience thus far indicates that a "generalized" scheme is not likely to be either uniform or generous.[17] And, of course, if tariff advantages for the LDCs were to be continued, tariffs among the rich countries would have to be kept at levels high enough so that a tariff differential could apply to the poor countries. In other words, an inefficient system would have to be perpetuated in order to help make the developing countries somewhat less inefficient.

A programmed reduction of tariffs, eventually to zero, along with a dismantling of nontariff barriers (which are discussed in chapter 7) would offer more

17. The United States had not by early 1975 put its scheme into effect. The preferences provided by Japan and the European Community do not cover all commodities and contain many restrictions. A recent study concludes that the program ". . . is in practice a programme of 'aid' rather than 'trade.'. . . The revenue transfers flowing from the programme are estimated to be less than $100 million which are quite insignificant when compared with other . . . aid." Tracy Murray, "How Helpful Is the Generalised System of Preferences to Developing Countries?" *Economic Journal,* vol. 83 (June 1973), pp. 453, 455.

for the export potential of the LDCs than preferential arrangements have any likelihood of doing, and without the political and economic drawbacks of preferences. But preferences could be continued and made much less restrictive during the period of phased tariff reductions, or tariff cuts could be applied to the LDCs on an accelerated schedule. There is justifiable concern that the least developed of the poor countries will not benefit from a system that does not actively discriminate in their favor. The answer is that adequate aid programs are the best means for creating diversified and competitive production; and there is little to suggest that preferences have led to diversification or to efficiency.

Although agricultural protection has its most important effects on trade in products grown in the industrial countries, agricultural exports from LDCs are also hampered. A prime example has been sugar, which has been second or third among the internationally traded agricultural commodities and is crucial for the trade prospects of some of the newest and poorest, as well as some of the largest of the LDCs. It has also been a major and protected domestic crop in Europe and the United States. Trade in sugar has been subject to a complex of arrangements: the International Sugar Agreement, which has been relevant mainly to the small free market; the Commonwealth Sugar Agreement, which governed trade at fixed prices between the United Kingdom and its Commonwealth associates; the U.S. sugar legislation, which held a portion of the American market open to imports (usually at premium prices); and the European Community's internal system of a guaranteed price, which has led to so much production that the Community has been a sugar exporter in competition with such countries as Mauretania. In addition, the Soviet Union has had a purchase arrangement with Cuba.

The current period of abnormally high sugar prices unquestionably will lead to more investment and increased output in the tropical sugar-producing countries. In the United States the decision has been taken to experiment with a virtually free market in sugar,[18] and all LDC exporters will have the opportunity to compete in it. In the Lomé Convention, the European Community in effect has taken over the British Commonwealth sugar quota. It remains to be seen, however, whether the rich countries are prepared to provide adequate market access for tropical sugar over the longer term.

Proposals to link aid to the developing countries with reform of the monetary system have languished because definitive reform has been deferred. The most publicized of these proposals was to provide International Monetary

---

18. The U.S. Congress in June 1974 somewhat unexpectedly declined to renew the long-standing sugar legislation and the Ford administration has proceeded to administer its remaining authority over sugar on the most liberalized basis possible.

Fund (IMF) Special Drawing Rights (SDRs) to developing countries in larger amounts than would be justified under normal procedures. With flexible or floating exchange rates the rule, the general case for large issues of SDRs (to increase world liquidity) promised to be less pressing; but the oil-financing problem may bring the SDR question to the fore again as a way of financing the deficits of the very poor nations. Other monetary system approaches may be considered in due course. Thus, if the "overhang" of dollars in central bank reserves was to be funded—presumably turned over to the IMF in return for SDRs—one possibility would be for the IMF to pay a nominal interest rate on these new issues while the United States continued to pay the market rate for the dollars now in IMF hands; the interest differential would give the Fund substantial sums that could be used for development aid. Or government gold holdings could be exchanged for SDRs, and the Fund could engage in carefully timed sales of gold on the private market, with the profits going to an aid fund. These are not imminent possibilities, to be sure, but they may become practicable in the not distant future.

Plans for using the resources of the seabeds offer another opportunity for helping poor nations. The U.S. government made proposals to this end a few years ago, suggesting that the benefits of exploiting some of these resources be made available to the international community generally, rather than only to the exploiting nations. While American enthusiasm for these proposals has diminished, the idea may be worth reviving, but this, too, is for the future. The resources likely to be exploited in the near term clearly fall in areas under national control and jurisdiction.

Shorter-Range Measures

Other measures may hold greater promise for the near term; the rollover of external debts may be the only immediately feasible way to help some countries that are facing extraordinary balance-of-payments deficits. But none of this can substitute for more official aid. The latter is needed particularly by the countries that face the most serious problems—the so-called fourth world: India, Bangladesh, Sri Lanka, and many of the African and some of the Latin American countries. Others—such as Brazil, Mexico, Korea, and Taiwan—can be expected to make their own way, for the most part. But the countries that are the worst off need special help.

A consensus has been building up for greater multilateralism in the development aid process. Some 60 percent of development lending now goes through the World Bank agencies and the regional development banks. Bilateral programs are spread more widely. There are more lending nations, and their activities extend to more countries. The number of consortium arrangements has increased, and the requirements of debt rescheduling have led to joint action by creditors. The oil crisis has brought into being an IMF-IBRD Development Committee with a mandate which could lead to improved coordination between aid givers, including the oil-rich countries, and aid recipients. Also support for untied aid has grown, and this form of multilateral giving or lending would probably now be in effect if France and the United States alone had not stood out against it.

Of course, none of this is a substitute for a sufficient flow of resources to the poor countries, but it is an encouraging development nonetheless. Indeed, in all aspects of the North-South relationship, the developed countries must act together if they are to act effectively. When the question concerns agricultural trade, a multilateral access agreement will provide greater benefits to exporting countries and will be politically easier for the importing nations than unilateral measures can be. When it is a matter of imports of manufactures from the low-wage nations, none of the industrial countries alone can open its market. Unless development aid can be made more of a multinational affair, the tendency will be for the major donors to allow the quantity and quality of their aid to deteriorate to the level of the least generous among them. To be responsive to the real problems of the 1970s and 1980s, policies not only of the United States and Western Europe but also of Japan will have to be cooperative and coordinated in their North-South aspects as in other respects.

CHAPTER NINE

ATLANTIC RELATIONS: CHANGE TO WHAT?

It is hardly surprising that the relationship between North America and Western Europe is very different in the 1970s than it was in the 1950s or 1960s. The period since the end of World War II is already longer by nine years than the interim between the two great wars. Almost a generation has passed since the Marshall Plan was launched and since the long confrontation with the USSR began. The process of trying to construct a European Community has understandably preoccupied the Western European states. Japan, quite suddenly and startlingly, is a major power once more. The relative position of the United States in the world has declined and its leadership is no longer accepted unquestioningly by allies and friends abroad. Differences over the details of economic policy, which have always existed in transatlantic relations, have taken on new forms. In third areas of the world new issues have arisen toward which the United States and Western Europe have opposing positions. And it was inevitable that in a period of détente there should be grounds for doubt about military and security arrangements that, after all, date back more than twenty years to a very different era. Perhaps most important of all, on both sides of the Atlantic, domestic goals have become more urgent than in the years that were dominated by the East-West confrontation.

In these circumstances, the goal of an Atlantic community that would bind the United States and Western Europe in an ever closer association seems hopelessly out of reach. For it to be revived would require a crisis that threatened the security of the Atlantic countries more directly and fundamentally than any in the past.

But the opposing and radical idea of disengagement between the United States and Europe hardly seems more real. It is possible, but only remotely so, that a government could come to power in Washington determined to abandon what has been a cardinal feature of U.S. policy for twenty-five years—the preoccupation with European security. That Western Europe might achieve the degree of unity associated with a nation-state and choose to divorce itself from the relationship with America is even less probable.

In fact, governments on both sides of the Atlantic, whatever their rhetoric, have not acted as though either Atlantic community or European self-reliance and disengagement were genuine options. They have tried to deal with specific problems through existing institutions and to adjust the relative U.S. and European roles pragmatically to changing circumstances, doing whatever has seemed most likely to solve the problems at hand, but without any overall blueprint for a new Atlantic relationship.

Governments have been right to take this attitude. The time is not ripe either for a rebirth of Atlanticism or for a radical shift to European self-reliance. Pressed with sufficient tenacity, such pragmatic problem-solving has good prospects of success, in the existing European and Atlantic frameworks when warranted, but within wider groupings if necessary. Atlantic crises seem to generate a despairing view, particularly among intellectuals, that we face problems so nearly insoluble that only grand and dramatic initiatives can possibly set things right. Such initiatives are clearly infeasible in a period of weak governments and self-centered electorates on both sides of the Atlantic. But neither are they clearly necessary. Sustained problem-solving will do more than grandiose blueprints to meet present needs. The problems are serious, but not unmanageable.

Immediate Defense Problems

Turning to the central question of Atlantic defense, we have seen that there are many reasons why basic changes in NATO planning and deployment are needed. One important reason is the prospect of a growing shortfall in U.S. and European troops for NATO. To assume that this can be prevented by maintaining Atlantic military manpower at present levels and increasing defense budgets is wishful thinking. The trend toward smaller armies is not only due to mounting expense. It also reflects deep-seated social phenomena and an altered perception of the military role that are not easily overridden. To assume, on the other hand, that the problem can be overcome by independent European initiatives is even more fanciful. No substitute for a joint U.S.-European defense effort is in sight.

In the United States, the idea is deeply embedded that a U.S. government should be ready to risk war to prevent the Soviet Union from gaining political control over Western Europe by force. Because of this unprecedented commitment, it is wholly rational and indeed essential that the United States should be directly involved in decisions about the defense of Europe. If NATO did not exist for the purpose, something like it would have to be invented. Similarly, from a European point of view, the political realities are that the Soviet Union is prepared to devote considerably greater resources to military power than are the other European states and that the limits on the Western European defense effort are firmly rooted in European attitudes and political processes. The U.S. commitment to Europe's defense is therefore indispensable for balancing Soviet armed strength, and that commitment is believable and binding not because of the words, which are equivocal, but because of the American presence and participation in the North Atlantic Treaty Organization.

If Western policy eventually leads to a lessening of power disparities in Europe, through negotiations or otherwise, NATO in its present form may in due course become unnecessary and may even be replaced by East-West institutions and by understandings regarding European security. It is very early, however, to conclude that this time has arrived. Soviet military risk-taking in Europe is, to be sure, unlikely. It is only a reasonable caution, however, to note that the Soviet military establishment in Europe remains overwhelmingly strong, and that power relationships still matter. Former West German Chancellor Willy Brandt has not been the only one to point out that whether the movement toward détente in Central Europe goes forward on a sound base will depend to a large extent on whether East-West military power appears balanced in Europe.

If neither greater Atlantic interdependence and effort nor much greater European self-reliance is feasible, to stand pat on present NATO policies and dispositions would also hardly be realistic. NATO military arrangements will have to be revised in view of the trend toward declining military manpower noted above. Important steps can be taken to this end, notably by shifting to a short-war strategy and reducing support and long-lead reserve forces accordingly. To economize on manpower within a viable structure of conventional defense would be in line with public sentiment and political reality in both North America and Europe. If, in addition, efforts were made to show that the Eurogroup could integrate logistics, equipment, and doctrine more closely among the European NATO members, and if these steps were accompanied by a somewhat improved and more lasting program for U.S.-European burden-sharing, NATO would have been made more durable, and the U.S. political problem in maintaining a substantial, if somewhat reduced, level of forces in Europe made somewhat easier. These tasks are not beyond doing; and they can be prosecuted through existing institutions.

These institutions are not, however, immutable. A trend toward greater defense concert among the members of the European Community—which happen to be the European nations most directly concerned with the central front—would make the Atlantic defense connection more viable over the longer term. It should be encouraged, even if it means reduced European defense purchases in the United States and a less dominant U.S. role in NATO military planning. Over the longer term, NATO might revolve increasingly around the connection between such a European defense grouping and the United States, with special arrangements being made to assure continuing defense ties with other NATO countries under the NATO umbrella. But these are long-term directions. The immediate need is to grapple with pressing problems through the policy changes described above.

These changes require political direction and decision. The NATO military leadership is not disposed to innovation; in any case it cannot move further or faster than its political guidance and support will allow. If NATO's problems are serious enough, then means must be found to focus on them at a high political level and to give clear directions to the military command for needed change. If this is not done, declining levels of military manpower and increasing pressures for reducing U.S. forces in Europe could fulfill the prophecy of the recently retired chairman of NATO's Military Committee that NATO will become only a rather expensive military museum. And whatever the military import of an erosion of NATO ground strength, the resulting political environment would make it increasingly difficult to go forward with negotiating East-West détente, building a viable European Community, and strengthening U.S.-European economic cooperation.

Immediate Political Problems

The same need for the pragmatic approach rather than grand design can be discerned in the political field. There are three categories of problems: East-West relations, policies toward third world areas, and bilateral relations between the United States and the European Community.

East-West Relations

Misgivings about the dangers of multilateral East-West negotiations appear to have been greatly overdrawn. The conference on European security and the mutual force reduction talks have been marked by close and effective cooperation among the Western powers. If there are threats to Western unity in this kind of exercise, they have not been apparent so far. Nor is it clear that either exercise will require creating new Atlantic or European political institutions; existing ones seem adequate. The main need is to get on with the business at hand. The greatest potential lies in the mutual force reduction talks. These could lead not only to some reduction in forces but also, and at least equally important, to negotiated agreements on safeguards against surprise attack and other measures to enhance stability in Europe. If agreement on mutual reductions cannot be reached, the United States might, by a modest unilateral move to cut its forces in Europe, explore the possibilities of a tacit process of U.S. action and Soviet counteraction in this field. But this would be a poor second, since it would presumably not be accompanied by the collateral measures mentioned above.

U.S.-Soviet strategic and other bilateral negotiations are a more sensitive area. The fear that superpower deals will be made at Western Europe's expense probably cannot be erased. It will haunt the Atlantic relationship as long as Europe is dependent on U.S. military support. At the same time, there is no way to change the fact that every U.S. administration—and especially every U.S. president—will have overriding domestic as well as foreign policy reasons for pursuing direct discussions with the leadership of the Soviet Union and now of China. By all accounts, the risks of critical interallied misunderstanding have been avoided thus far in the U.S.-Soviet strategic arms limitation talks. The saving device, it is said, has been to give prompt and full information to the Western European allies. Whether this will be enough if and when the talks grapple with issues of more direct concern to Europe than those that have arisen in SALT thus far is uncertain. But a better remedy is not at hand.

Policies toward Third World Areas

U.S. and European policies toward third areas, by contrast, may not become compatible no matter how much consultation takes place. For a time after World War II it was an article of faith that the foreign policies of the Atlantic countries toward these areas ought to be concerted. At first the dominance of U.S. power and the perceived Soviet threat made this a feasible goal, as in Korea. But a declining U.S. role and changing perceptions of the Soviet Union have altered this; General de Gaulle's challenge to U.S. policy in Southeast Asia and elsewhere was more a symptom than the cause of a growing European unwillingness to follow the U.S. lead. So it seems likely that the United States and Western Europe will continue to diverge from time to time in their approaches to third areas where they consider important interests to be at stake.

This prospect cannot be changed merely by prescribing more consultation, useful though this may be in forestalling unnecessary confrontation. For example, European and U.S. attitudes toward the Middle East reflect different domestic pressures. No U.S. administration will be as indifferent to Israeli concerns as certain European governments have shown themselves to be; and few European governments can afford to be as brave in the face of Arab oil pressure as the United States. These conflicting views on the Middle East may be duplicated in other areas. If there is eventually a black-white confrontation in southern Africa, it is hard to believe that former colonial powers in Europe and a United States that faces serious domestic racial problems will reach identical conclusions.

Given these circumstances, it is well to ask whether U.S.-European unity in policy toward third areas is a feasible goal. It may be the greater part of wisdom to recognize that major differences are natural and inevitable at this stage of the political development of the two sides, rather than a sign of failure. If this can be made clear to the general public, it may be easier to prevent likely recurring disagreements about policy toward the Middle East, Africa, and other regions of more or less common concern from disrupting Atlantic economic and defense cooperation.

Bilateral U.S.-European Relations

In the economic field also, a pragmatic problem-solving approach seems indicated; no opportunity for dramatic new realignments is evident. The management of problems in the evolving U.S.-European Community relationship is likely to be chronically troublesome. Few Community supporters are free of the lingering suspicion that Washington will one day exert its influence to attempt to break up the Community if it cannot dominate the latter's policy. On the other hand, a "Europe" that is supposed to deal as a whole with the United States has a large fictional element, at least as far as questions outside of the commercial policy field are concerned. Inevitably, even on matters clearly within the Community's jurisdiction, U.S. officials and politicians will seek to make arrangements directly with member governments—or try to influence the Community's decisions through bilateral negotiations and pressures. This happens not out of any general malevolence—even if a few Americans might be happy to see the Community dissolved—but because the quickest, surest, or only way to achieve results may be to deal on occasion with the member states rather than to wait for the cumbersome Community procedures to produce a mandate that then takes on the characteristics of statutory law.

Tensions of this kind between the United States and the Community will persist. The Community will not be decisively unified at any foreseeable date, and the United States will not cease dealing on occasion with individual European countries on a bilateral basis as well as with the Community. Improved transatlantic consultation procedures that permit U.S.-Community discussions to take place before Community decisions are made will not make the problem go away; at best, they reduce its scope and abrasiveness.

Over the longer term, Europeans will probably come to see that their view of U.S. motivations for wanting to break up the Community has been greatly exaggerated. At the heart of U.S. policy toward Europe since World War II has been the perceived need for a permanent French-German reconciliation. How the United States could profit from destruction of the Community, which has been able to accommodate within it the two ancient European rivals, is far from clear. U.S. irritation with certain aspects of Community policy may be perennial, but deliberate hostility toward the idea of European integration makes no sense. These considerations should eventually become evident to Europeans, and they will be the more likely to mitigate European concerns in the degree that they clearly guide the United States in any response to U.S.-European disagreements.

Immediate Prospects

In the meantime, money, trade, and investment—and now energy—will continue to be the subjects of transatlantic dialogue and sometimes disagreement. Differences between the views of the United States and some or all Community members on economic matters will remain. Still, although negotiation will be paralleled by occasional verbal exchanges, it is clear that no one is likely to favor a disruption of economic interdependence, however awkward interdependence may sometimes be. For from a domestic point of view, individuals and groups can easily be disadvantaged—or appear to be disadvantaged— by transactions that involve other nations. In democratic societies, pressures to seal off or to manipulate the international economy—for reasons of social justice or to help particularly vulnerable groups—are normal and rather constant. And they are part of every democratic politician's life. They cannot and will not always be resisted in any country, but neither have they to date overcome on any large scale and over any sustained period the opposing interests of powerful groups in the benefits of a functioning international economic system.

In the economic, as in the defense field, however, specific changes are needed—for example, movement toward an agricultural compromise that will eventually allow a better allocation of farm resources in Europe and North America and the building of international food reserves, a reduction in tariff and nontariff barriers, joint action to increase energy supplies and reduce consumption, more effective concert on the recycling problem, and joint aid to the less developed countries—particularly aid that will help them to increase food production.

If there is cause for concern, it is that these matters may not have been addressed with the urgency that they deserve. Steps are being taken to deal with some issues; but all observers agree that there has been considerable lethargy. Troubles have arisen in new fields—energy, for example—and have dragged on for a long time in others, such as agricultural trade. Continuing drift can only make matters worse. The United States, to be sure, has recognized this danger. To have proclaimed 1973 as "the year of Europe" was more than faintly patronizing; and the arbitrary time period was mere sloganeering. But the conception was right insofar as it meant that political leadership should focus on the stubborn, unresolved questions in American-European affairs. This is so, first, because these questions ultimately have a large domestic quotient. Presidents and prime ministers are best situated to judge what is politically feasible, that is, how far political mandates at home can be stretched to make international bargains. Second, because the issues are in many respects technical and complex, and even somewhat shady, the participation of political leaders may well raise the level of debate and emphasize to the various publics involved the essential commonality of their interests. It is inherently absurd, for instance, that disputes about agricultural policy could be thought of as bearing on the survival of an alliance that all parties consider of vital security interest. Yet problems of this kind have not been resolved in any lasting way at official levels, despite years of effort.

So periodic and even frequent consultation at the highest political levels may help to break some of the deadlocks, just as the 1971 Smithsonian agreement was made possible by prior meetings between the U.S. President and the British and French prime ministers. It is doubtful, however, that much of substance can come from statements of broad Atlantic objectives, such as the one made in June 1974. The effort to get such an agreed statement was bound to produce limited and platitudinous results, if only because European politicians are divided and unsure about the future of Atlanticism and American leadership must act within sharp political limits. Even though preoccupation with more or less eloquent communiqués may be harmless enough, progress toward resolving specific disputed issues will matter more than expressions of general principles and long-term goals.

This is the more true since the future is unlikely to conform to either the European or the Atlantic vision that must shadow any further joint declara-

LEWIS AND CLARK COLLEGE LIBRARY
PORTLAND, OREGON 97219

tions. A dynamic process is under way among the democratic powers, the Soviet Union, and China, and, perhaps even more important, between North and South. Its predictable result is that national and regional interests will increasingly be engaged with broader, more nearly global interests, and that the responsibility for guiding these interests toward sensible accommodation will fall often and heavily not only on the United States and the EC but also on Japan and perhaps eventually the Soviet Union. The need for these developed countries to play a leading role in the collective management of economic and environmental problems in a crowded planet is likely to be a greater challenge even than containing the threat of nuclear war, and it cannot be met by Atlantic action alone.

More and more it seems likely, therefore, that the Atlantic relationship will merge into a broader international grouping, where the technical skills and the productive capacities of the affluent nations will have to be mobilized for common and compelling ends, including cooperation in the development of less affluent countries. If this happens, it will not be the end of the Atlantic vision but its natural and necessary extension. The best way to prepare for this movement is not now radically to reshape existing U.S.-European institutions and arrangements, which will eventually be outmoded by wider trends in any case, but to make within these institutions the changes in current policy that will be needed to cope with specific problems as we make our way toward a larger community of developed societies.

The actions now required by this strategy are not infeasible. In defense, politics, and economics specific changes in present policies can be discerned which are within the political capacity of present leadership on both sides of the Atlantic, weakened and distracted though it may be. Restructuring NATO forces to cope with declining military manpower; pressing ahead with East-West negotiations, while recognizing the limits of common political action toward third areas; and action to reduce agricultural and other trade barriers, increase energy supplies, and concert on more effective aid to the less developed countries—none of these are beyond the bounds of present political reality. They would not, of course, provide the major restructuring of international institutions that may eventually be needed. But they would see us through the present period of difficulty and uncertainty until the larger needs—which go far beyond the bounds of the Atlantic connection—come to be more confidently discerned and more widely accepted by electorates in both Europe and North America.

1013

DATE

'82

Lewis and Clark College - Watzek Library
D1065.U5 T73   wmain
Trezise, Philip H./The Atlantic connecti

3 5209 00372 1517